ELLIE BEAVIS

find it - keep it - live it

WWW.ELLIEBEAVIS.COM

MW01110424

JOY! Find it, Keep it, Live it
by Ellie Beavis

Copyright © 2005 Ellie Beavis. All rights reserved.

1st printing July 2005

PRINTED IN THE UNITED STATES OF AMERICA BY
Birmingham Press, San Diego, California

COVER PHOTOGRAPHY
David Buranich

COPYRIGHT & PUBLISHING ADMINISTRATION
Powerborn
631 Via Paraiso
Corona, California USA 92882
Phone (951)739-0634 Fax (714)464-4171
www.EllieBeavis.com

All rights reserved. No part of this book may be reproduced in any form without written permission from the publisher.

All Scripture quotations, unless otherwise indicated, are taken from the Holy Bible, New International Version. NIV Copyright 1973, 1978, 1984 by International Bible Society. Used by Permission of Zondervan Publishing House. All rights reserved.

Scripture taken from THE MESSAGE Copyright 1993, 1994, 1995, 1996, 2000, 2001, 2002. Used by permission of NavPress Publishing Group.

Scripture quotations marked NLT are taken from the Holy Bible, New Living Translation, copyright 1996 Used by permission of Tyndale Hose Publishers Inc. Wheaton, Illinois 60189. All rights reserved.

Library of Congress Cataloging-in-Publication Data
Beavis, Ellie.
        JOY! Find it, Keep it, Live it / Ellie Beavis
        p.   cm.
        ISBN 978-1-888741-05-6 (sc)
        1. Christian life—Biblical teaching.   2. Quality of life—Religious
        3. Self-actualization / Maturation (Psychology)   I. Title
        248.4 BEA —dc22   2005

9 8 7 6 5 4 3 2 1

This book is dedicated with all my love to
Wes, David and Zachary.

Thank you for filling my life with love,
laughter and joy.

Contents

⸎

Introduction 7

1. Complete Joy 9

2. Choose Joy 21

3. Praise On! 33

4. Find the Fun 43

5. A Changed Perspective 51

6. Look Up! 63

7. Enjoy the Ride 71

8. No Place I'd Rather Be 81

9. Uniquely You 89

10. Good Medicine 99

11. Wide Open Spaces 109

12. Deflating Joy 119

13. Fading Joy 129

14. Overflowing Joy 139

15. A Life of Joy 147

Introduction

I have spent the past ten years living in what is described as a highly affluent part of the world. People seem to have it all: big homes, nice vehicles, and expensive vacations. People enjoy wonderful weather, good health and the convenience of having the best retail stores just a short drive away. People seem to have so much.

Yet, in a place of plenty, a sense of joy seems strangely absent. Anti-depressant medications are prescribed for millions of people each year. Cases of teenagers with depression are increasing. Even children are diagnosed as suffering different forms of depression. It seems we have an epidemic of unhappy people.

Cases of clinical depression may be the result of chemical imbalances, genetic, biological or environmental factors. It is evident that medications can provide some relief. For some people, medications may be the solution.

However, everyone can't be suffering from the same medical malaise. Are we all in need of a prescribed pick-me-up? Is a vacation, a new car, or a trip to the mall the best way to experience joy?

I believe that we all have days, even weeks, of battling despair or hopelessness. For whatever reason, we find ourselves feeling 'down' or 'blue'. But I also believe that, too easily, we overlook the spiritual solution in our quest for an external remedy. For God offers the best means to counteract the downward drag of life. He gives us joy beyond anything that can be experienced, purchased, or prescribed.

In a culture that seeks answers in materialism and medication, I have sought to understand what God's Word has to say about joy, how to find that joy and once found, how to keep it and live it.

My prayer is that this book will help you to discover or re-discover this wonderful, God-given facet to life; and that your joy will overflow and impact those around you.

Ellie Beavis

1

complete Joy

Do not be dejected and sad for the joy
of the Lord is your strength.
Nehemiah 8:10 (NLT)

One summer, my family ventured out on a camping
trip. It was not so much the call of the wild that
beckoned us. It was more that it was an inexpensive
way for a large family to take a vacation. My parents
purchased a designer tent with attachable curtains,
zip-in bedrooms and lightweight aluminum poles.

That summer, we loaded the family sedan: my parents,
my brother and two sisters, my mother's step-sister, a
foster child who was spending a year with the family,
and me. That's eight bodies, eight sleeping bags and a

tent that sleeps eight, packed into a car and box-trailer.

As is so often the case with family vacations, it did not go as planned. One evening, a coastal storm ripped through the camping grounds. And how it ripped. Gale force winds pounded the coastline for hours.

Despite our valiant efforts, the tent was shredded and collapsed into a sodden heap. My family sought shelter with an old family friend who lived in a town fifteen miles away. Eight wet, miserable people arrived on her doorstep to wait out the storm. Our friend gave us a place to sleep and some dry clothes that she had been preparing to drop into the Salvation Army.

The next morning, we returned to the camping ground on a salvage mission. We picked up the drenched sleeping bags, the camping equipment, and our poor excuse for a tent and loaded it back into the car and trailer. Yet, re-packing wet gear proved challenging and we discovered we could no longer all fit in the car. So my parents sent my sister, my brother and my aunt home on the train.

Feeling despondent and weary, the rest of us set out on the journey home. Not only did we feel defeated, we looked ridiculous. The clothes intended for the Salvation Army were old and ill-fitting. My father, who is six feet tall, was wearing trousers intended for someone much shorter and much broader.

Complete Joy

Breaking up our journey, we stopped at a rest stop and my Dad, an educated and contemplative man, proceeded to skip across the park. It was so out of character and highly entertaining! We laughed so hard and, in that moment, my Dad showed us how to experience joy in the midst of our difficulties.

Joy is like that. No matter what a person may be experiencing, whatever challenge they may be facing, joy can still be present. Unlike happiness, which may come and go, joy has the ability to be constant and lasting.

I would consider myself a happy person. I am more likely to be up than down. I tend to be positive rather than negative. I am more phlegmatic than melancholic. I like to smile. I love to laugh. I prefer comedy to soap operas, and gospel music to the blues.

Yes, I am happy most of the time. But happiness can be fleeting. It can come and go according to the events of a day or the date on a calendar. If things are going well, then happiness abounds.

A new pair of shoes can be reason to be happy. If I spend time with family or friends, then I am happy. If I have successfully maintained my goal weight, I am very happy. Gain a few pounds, and my happiness quickly evaporates.

Happiness has to do with what happens. I'm sure the similar spelling of these words is no accident! Happiness is based in external experiences.

We may spend a lot of time and energy in the pursuit of something that we believe will make us happy and yet, happiness may be ever elusive. It is unpredictable. It is superficial.

Whereas the word 'happy' refers to a temporary emotion, 'joy' describes a state of being. I may be a happy person but more than that, I am a person who has joy. As pastor and author, Henri J.M. Nouwen states: "Joy is not the same as happiness. We can be unhappy about many things, but joy can still be there. . ."

Regardless of whether a summer vacation has been ruined, a financial setback has interrupted life, or things have not gone my way, the presence of joy is constant. Joy is lasting and steady.

Joy enables me to rise above my current circumstances because joy is not about what I have but who I know. It is founded in a relationship with God. As Dr. Robert Schuller states, "Joy is not the absence of suffering. It is the presence of God."

Abiding Joy

The words of Jesus in John 15 clearly establish the means to joy. It describes a state of dependence in which God is the vine and we are the branches. Without that connection, we are without our source of life. It is a dependency in which we acknowledge that, apart from Him, we can do nothing (John 15:5). As the Psalmist David wrote in Psalm 16: "You are my Lord; apart from you I have no good thing" (Psalm 16:2).

It is in this place where joy is found. Jesus tells his disciples,

> "If you obey my commands, you will remain
> in my love, just as I have obeyed my Father's
> commands and remain in his love. I have
> told you this so that my joy may be in you
> and that your joy may be made complete."
> (John 15:10-11)

This complete joy is what emerges from a connection to our Creator. David describes this connection in Psalm 16: "You have made known to me the path of life; you will fill me with joy in your presence" (Psalm 16:11).

JOY!

In his book *Walking Wisely*, Pastor Charles Stanley writes:

> "When we know with certainty that God is in control, that He loves us beyond measure, and that He is at work in our lives, we have the genuine capacity to praise and thank God even in the midst of the most dire, discouraging or depressing times."[1]

In other words, when I view every relationship, every challenge, and every situation from a perspective of how God is at work in my life, my joy remains intact.

Joy is Big

Joy has just three letters. It seems like such a little word. Yet, joy is listed in the spiritual fruit as found in Galatians: ". . . the fruit of the spirit is love, *joy*, peace, patience, kindness, goodness, faithfulness, gentleness and self-control" (Galatians 5:22-2, italics added). As much as I may struggle with things like self-control or patience, I need to nurture joy in my life. I need to provide the conditions that will protect my joy because my joy is often under threat.

The thief who "comes only to steal and kill and

destroy" (John 10:10) has his sights set on our joy. What is it about joy that makes it a target for attack from the thief, Satan? He knows something that we often fail to remember: joy is big.

In Nehemiah 8:10, we read: "the joy of the Lord is your strength." Joy is where the strength of the Lord can be found in my life. See, that's big. In other words, where my joy is, you'll find my strength— the strength that comes from God. If my joy is diminished, then my strength falters. No wonder Satan wants to steal, kill and destroy my joy.

Pastor Joel Osteen, explains in his book, *Your Best Life Now*:

> "We need to understand that the enemy is not really after your dreams, your health or your finances. He's primarily after your joy. The Bible says that 'the joy of the Lord is your strength' and your enemy knows if he can deceive you into living down in the dumps and depressed, then you are not going to have the necessary strength— physically, emotionally, or spiritually— to withstand his attacks. You will be vulnerable and beatable."[2]

JOY!

During our first year of marriage, Wes was an intern at a church. The church provided us with the back half of an old house adjacent to the church property. Along one side of the house was a shortcut to the stores of the city's main street. Even though it was a private yard, there was a constant stream of mostly young people making their way through the side yard.

One afternoon, I was at the kitchen table eating an apple and studying for an upcoming college exam when I heard a noise. I entered the bedroom from where the noise had come. There, by the vanity, was a teenage girl rummaging through the drawers. We were both startled by the unexpected appearance of another person. She jumped out the open window and started running.

Not knowing what else to do, I jumped out the window and chased after her. Wanting to scare off the assailant, I threw my apple at her. Although I missed hitting her with my weapon of choice, I felt like I had succeeded in making sure she would not be back.

Returning to the house, I noticed a crumpled ten dollar bill on the ground. It had been on my dresser and the young girl, maybe fearing being caught (or the wrath of my apple toss), dropped what she had stolen.

If only it were always that easy to get back our possessions after they have been stolen. Talk to anyone who has had their home or car broken into, and one of the first things that is required by the police is a list of all that is stolen. Even though they may attempt to list every item, months later they'll be searching for a missing CD or piece of jewelry, and suddenly remember that it, too, must have been stolen.

Stolen joy is hard to recover. Sometimes we don't even know when it was taken. The first indication that our joy has been plundered may be when we notice that despair or despondency have moved in.

We need to keep our joy safe from the enemy. We need to lock the windows, lock the doors and activate the burglar alarm. We need to keep our joy secure.

Safeguarding Your Joy

When I was eleven years old, the church my family was attending had guest singers visit from the United States. The twin sisters were sharing their musical talents with churches around Australia. These singing sisters with their American accents intrigued my friend, Sonia, and me. They shared a little song that I still remember probably because Sonia and I would sing trying our best to sound like them. To this day, I can give my best impression of an American accent when I sing: "Joy is the flag flown high from the castle of my heart."

This picture of my heart as a castle brings to mind the words of Proverbs 4: "Above all else, guard your heart for it is the wellspring of life" (Proverbs 4:23). In other words, our heart is like the central command post that directs how we live life. It is the place where our desires and attitudes originate.

Just as a guard protects the entrance to a castle or a palace to determine whether an approaching visitor is friendly or hostile, we need to guard our hearts to determine whether what we allow to enter is going to be helpful or harmful.

We need to keep watch and protect our hearts from the things that may threaten our joy and therefore, drain our strength. We need to safeguard our joy from attack and from those things that can too readily cause our joy to be depleted. Difficult circumstances can sap our joy. Fear, anxiety and busyness can extinguish our joy. Keeping watch for these threats to our joy is a good defense.

Yet, as any coach will tell you, a good defense also needs a good offense in order to win a game. A good offense means we will do those things that will restore and strengthen our joy. A changed perspective, a spirit of contentment, gratitude and seeking a good support system will provide an offensive good enough to defeat any enemy with an intent to steal our joy.

In this way, no matter what life may bring, we can emerge with our joy intact. We will fly the flag of joy as evidence to the world that our King is in residence. This joy will be our strength and we will be able to withstand any attack. Our joy will be complete.

2

Choose Joy

It is important to become aware that at
every moment of our life we have an
opportunity to choose joy.
Henri J.M. Nouwen

It would be true to say that I am a planner. I usually
have a plan in place or I like to know what the plan
will be. In many ways, it is a good attribute to have
because with good planning, I have accomplished some
significant things. But, it can have its downside.

Frankly, I don't like surprises. If there is a surprise, it
means something in my plan has to be re-planned.

On my last birthday, my friends Angie and Jo
planned a surprise breakfast for me at Laguna Beach.

With my husband and sons as co-conspirators, they arranged to pick me up, or should I say kidnap me, from the grocery store.

My plan was to celebrate my birthday with a special breakfast with Wes and our sons, David and Zachary, at one of our favorite restaurants. On the way to the restaurant, Zachary, my ten year old who deserves an Academy award for his performance, announced that we needed new batteries for the digital camera.

Wes stopped by the grocery store and gave me instructions about exactly which batteries to purchase. I'm sure as I stepped out of the car I grumbled about why I had to get out and buy the batteries since it was my birthday.

Having purchased the batteries as per Wes' instructions, I exited the store to find Angie's car parked where I expected to see Wes. Adding to my confusion, Angie and Jo were beckoning me to jump in their car.

I was so surprised and just a little shaken by the turn of events. Yet my excitement was soon replaced with many questions: Where were we going? Where was Wes? Did he know about the surprise? Did the boys know I wasn't going to breakfast with them? How long would we be gone for?

Angie and Jo laughed at my questions which were

my desperate attempt to get on board with a plan that was not my own. After I resolved that they had taken good care of all the planning, I relaxed and had a wonderful and memorable birthday.

It is good when an unexpected plan brings something pleasant. It is easy to experience joy when a surprise brings something good. But when our plans are unexpectedly interrupted by something bad, our joy can easily drain away.

Sorrow Lasts for the Night

Undoubtedly, we have all had times when life has not gone as planned. But more than just an interruption or hiccup, we may experience tragedy and loss. In those times, we may want to wallow in our despair, and to hide in our grief. When tragedy strikes, we are perfectly justified in feeling sorrow and sadness.

In fact, sometimes it is essential to express our sorrow. Repressed grief is not healthy and so we do need to mourn. As Ecclesiastes 3:4 states, there is a "time to weep and a time to laugh, a time to mourn and a time to dance."

When David was eighteen months old, I calculated

that it would be a good time to have another baby. Wes and I had waited seven years before having David and, in keeping with my plan, I decided that the ideal age difference between the children would be two and a half years, lest life be too chaotic. Yes, it just required good planning, or so I thought. I was thrilled when I discovered that I was pregnant and that the baby's due date would fit perfectly into my plan.

When I was fourteen weeks pregnant, my plans were upended. I noticed a little spotting so I went to see a doctor at the medical clinic responsible for patients with a specific type of medical insurance. I was assured all was fine.

As the days passed, it became clear to me that all was not fine. I made an appointment with another doctor. He immediately sent me for an ultrasound, which confirmed that the baby had died.

I was scheduled for surgery the next day. The receptionist at the hospital told me to be there at 8 a.m. The doctor who was to perform the surgery did not get to the hospital until 5 p.m. I was given the only available bed on the same floor as the maternity patients.

It was a miserable day. For nine hours, I heard new mothers tending to their new babies. Visitors, laden with flowers and gifts, dropped in to see newborn grandchildren, nieces and nephews. From time to time, a nurse would stop by my room and apologize for the confusion with the scheduling of my surgery. I spent my hours grieving for a baby I would never know and whose birth I would never celebrate.

After the surgery, I was wheeled into my room and I wept again at the finality of the surgery. And then, I had enough of being in that room.

The nurse informed me that I could leave as soon as I had something to eat and showered. I was determined to leave that place behind. So, mustering all my strength to overcome the nausea and light-headedness, I ate something and walked to the shower. I felt myself on the verge of passing out but knew I needed to get out of there and go home.

In the months that followed, I asked God, 'Why?' on more than one occasion. While I grieved from time to time, I kept a mental picture of me leaving that hospital room, closing the door on sorrow and turning towards God. As the words of the Bible reminded me:

> "We are hard pressed on every side, but not crushed; perplexed but not in despair; persecuted, but not abandoned; struck down but not destroyed" (2 Corinthians 4:8).

I held onto the knowledge that God had not abandoned me and that He was faithful and loving. I found comfort in my belief that "in all things God works for the good of those who love him" (Romans 8:28). It was that re-assurance that enabled me to choose joy rather than sorrow. Eighteen months later, I gave to birth to a very healthy, ten pound boy! We named him Zachary which means 'God remembered'.

When we find ourselves in a place where sorrow is overwhelming, we need to remember the words of Psalm 30:5: "Weeping may remain for a night, but rejoicing comes in the morning." In other words, sorrow lasts only for the night. It is temporary. Of course, it often feels like the morning will never come.

Some years ago, Wes thought a romantic getaway was needed. I organized the babysitter, he was in charge of booking the accommodations. Wes thought a drive into Mexico would be an adventure because he had heard resort quality accommodations were available for much less money than in California.

We followed the coast into Mexico and reached Ensenada. Wes made some enquiries at some of the hotels. It was not going to be as cheap as he had anticipated. After a walk around the marketplace, I was ready to drive back to San Diego. Wes, ever the adventurer, wanted to keep hunting for that 'great deal'.

By now, it was late afternoon and I was anxious to find a place to stay. We came to a big hotel right on the beach with a world famous seafood restaurant. Wes enquired about the availability of rooms that fit within our limited budget. There were none.

The hotel manager could see our plight and offered an alternative. Next to the hotel was a small garden with a trailer (in Australia, it would be called a caravan). She said we could have it for the night for just forty dollars. Wes jumped at it, much to my dismay.

It was the saddest, most dilapidated trailer I had ever seen. It was tiny. The floors had been warped by the damp, and the door could not be locked. There was an ironing board attached to the outside wall. The bathroom was no bigger than a bathroom on an airplane. This was no hotel room.

Wes and I ate dinner at the restaurant. Midway through the meal, the manager brought us candles as she had forgotten to tell us that there was no electricity connected to the trailer. A few moments later, she brought complimentary coffee and liqueur. I think she was beginning to feel sorry for us.

That night, we laid on top of the bed covers, wide-eyed listening to every new noise. After midnight, the restaurant staff gathered on the other side of the fence drinking and talking loudly. Of course, I had no idea what they were saying as they were speaking Spanish. I imagined the worst. It was a long, sleepless night.

We waited anxiously for the sun to rise. As soon as there was enough sunlight, we got up, loaded the car and drove back to California. It was the longest and least romantic night of our marriage.

There is nothing worse than waking in the middle of the night and feeling anxious. If you have ever settled a frightened child during the night, it may be difficult to convince them that there is nothing to fear. To a child, the night harbors many scary things.

Likewise, the long hours of darkness may cause our anxieties to loom larger and seem more intimidating. We can be overwhelmed with worries and fear during the night. Life with God means that no matter how dark the night may be, "joy cometh in the morning" (Psalm 30:5 KJV).

In the same way that the sunlight breaks through the darkness to bring the dawn, we can be sure that after a time of sorrow, joy will be restored. It may seem like a long night, but the morning light will break through the darkness. Joy will return.

Focus on Joy

There are times when our reserves of joy seem almost dry. For whatever reasons or circumstances, it seems joy is hidden beneath our clouds of despair. In those times, we need to follow the example of Jeremiah, the prophet.

For forty years, Jeremiah warned people who had rejected God of their impending punishment. He was the bearer of bad news and he was often persecuted because of his message. Such was his job that Jeremiah is often referred to as 'the weeping prophet'. He is the writer of a book in the bible called Lamentations. That name alone should give an insight into the tone of his messages.

In Lamentations 3, Jeremiah describes his despairing condition. These are some of his statements: "I am the man who has seen affliction" (vs.1), "I became the laughingstock of all my people" (vs. 14), "I have been deprived of peace; I have forgotten what prosperity is" (vs.17), and then he declares, "my soul is downcast within me" (vs.20). On hearing these sentiments, a therapist may have quickly prescribed something to lift Jeremiah's spirits.

However, just as it seems that Jeremiah's sadness and grief is too much to bear, he writes these wonderful words:

> "Yet, this I call to mind and therefore I have hope: Because of the Lord's great love we are not consumed, for his compassions never fail. They are new every morning; great is your faithfulness." (Lamentations 3:21-23)

Better than reaching for something to improve his mood, Jeremiah counters his despair with hope.

It is almost as if Jeremiah was traveling on his train of thoughts and he was headed to Misery City and Depressionville. He had been expressing his hardships and lamenting his condition. But with the phrase, "yet this I call to mind," he disembarked from that train and changed direction. It seems Jeremiah made a calculated decision to change his focus from his condition, to focus on the love, compassion, and faithfulness of God.

It is easy to focus on our despair and our difficulties. In fact, it takes no effort to focus on all that is wrong with our lives. It seems our natural inclination will lead us to be despondent and depressed. Often, we can just wake up in that state. And in that defeated state, we can easily fall prey to the enemy who wants to steal our joy and weaken us.

Choose Joy

There are times in our life when we just have to resolve to be joyful. Despite the downward drag of our natures, we need to counter with a joyful spirit. It may take effort; it may even require a little force. But we need to follow Jeremiah's lead and state, "yet this I call to mind." In other words, this is what I will focus on. I will focus on God's mercies and His unfailing love. I will focus on the joy of the Lord, my strength. And I will choose joy.

3

Praise On!

On your feet now— applaud God! Bring a gift of
laughter, sing yourselves into his presence.
Psalm 100 (The Message)

Recently, I upgraded my old cell phone for a new
camera phone. My kids were thrilled. Zachary quickly
figured out how to use the camera, schedule events
and play the free games. None of those new features
were of particular interest to me. What I was most
excited about was being able to select ring tones for my
friends.

Depending on who is calling, my phone plays the
melody which I have selected for that person from the
list of free sample sounds. If Wes calls, my phone plays

When the Saints Go Marching In. If my sons call me from the home phone, my cell phone plays the theme song from *The Sting.* If my friend, Angie, calls then my phone starts playing the *Hallelujah* chorus. Each caller has their own theme song. Their presence is announced with a song.

Imagine if we did have our own personal theme song and that every room we entered, our theme song would announce our arrival. Like the familiar melody that announced the presence of the shark in the movie *Jaws,* we would immediately bring our atmosphere into a room. Of course, the song would need to say something about you and your personality. I would definitely want to select a song that is upbeat and fun: maybe Abba's, *Dancing Queen* or REM's *Shiny Happy People.*

Just as songs may set the atmosphere, songs can also relax you. When I am running, driving in the car, or working, I usually have music playing. It can make the running seem less tedious, the traffic seem less intense, and my work seem more enjoyable.

Sometimes, the lyrics and the melody of a song transport my mind to a different place. It may be that I recall hearing the song in a particular setting. A song from the eighties may remind me of my high school days. Another song will remind me of being in the home of my sister, Sue, and I can imagine myself sitting in her kitchen, drinking coffee, listening to music, and catching up.

While a song can represent you, relax you or remind you of another time or place, perhaps God's greatest intention for songs is to help restore in you a right frame of mind.

On days when I feel less joyful, my joy may continue to dissipate despite my best efforts to choose joy. In these times, it takes more than a concentrated focus and a decision to opt for joy. What is required is for me to do the opposite of what my feelings may be telling me. Rather than co-operating with my feelings, I have to move forward in my faith. I have to move in the direction of God. I need to "sing. . . [myself] into his presence" (Psalm 100:1 The Message).

A Garment of Praise

Isaiah, another prophet from the Old Testament, gives his job description in Isaiah 61. One of his tasks, he says, is "to comfort all who mourn and provide for those who grieve" (Isaiah 61:2-3). Part of that comfort and provision, according to Isaiah, was to give "a garment of praise instead of a spirit of despair" (Isaiah 61:3).

I like that analogy of praise as a piece of clothing. Just as we reach for a sweater or jacket, we can put on praise. It is a tangible act. Like putting on a piece of clothing, we can purposefully sing songs of praise.

Singing songs of praise to God means that instead of focusing on my feelings, I focus on the character of God; instead of limiting my sights to my present condition, I lift my eyes to consider the majesty of God.

The first praise song recorded in the Bible was sung by Miriam, Moses' sister. It was a song of praise celebrating God's deliverance of the people of Israel out of Egypt. After the people safely crossed through the Red Sea, God closed the sea and their pursuers were drowned. Miriam led the women in song saying:

> "Sing to the Lord for he is highly exalted.
> The horse and its rider he has hurled into
> the sea." (Exodus 15:21)

The Psalms are a collection of praise songs, many of them written by King David. In times of hardship and despair, King David wrote songs to lift his spirits and to remind himself of God's faithfulness. It was when King David was overwhelmed by his troubles, he wrote of God:

"He lifted me out of the slimy pit, out of
the mud and mire; he set my feet upon a
rock. . . he put a new song in my mouth, a
hymn of praise to our God." (Psalm 40:2-3)

In the midst of less than ideal circumstances, we
need to praise God. The prophet Habakkuk wrote a
song of praise which expressed his faith that, despite
his dire circumstances, such as crop failure, he would
rejoice. He writes:

"Though the fig tree does not bud and there
are no grapes on the vines, though the olive
crop fails and the fields produce no food,
though there are no sheep in the pen and no
cattle in the stalls, yet I will rejoice in the
Lord, I will be joyful in God my Savior."
(Habakkuk 3:17-18)

There may be times when I feel less joy. It may be
the result of a direct blow to my joy reserves because of
some tragedy. It may be the result of an attack from
the enemy. Sometimes, it may be that life has been
hectic and in the busyness of life, I have not taken the
time to replenish my joy. It is then that I need to reach
for the garment of praise.

On those days when I need to cover myself with
praise, I will intentionally listen to and, if I am in my

car, sing songs that praise God. If David and Zack are in the car, I have to sing on the inside lest my efforts are met with cries of protest and pleas to stop embarrassing them!

As I focus on the words of the songs, my mind is transported beyond the mire of my current condition. Praise turns my eyes from my situation to His glory. A few songs later and I am no longer singing the blues but singing, "I'm trading my sorrows, I'm trading my shame, I'm laying them down for the joy of the Lord."[1]

There may be days when we reach for this garment of praise automatically. We may start the day feeling full of praise in anticipation of the day ahead. There may be other times when we have to intentionally reach for it because the conditions look less than ideal. Chances are, it is the time when we need it the most.

Rejoice Always

Two weeks after immigrating to the United States, Wes developed an abscessed tooth. He had been receiving treatment before we moved from Australia but suddenly, the infection re-developed. We managed to get referred to a dentist. The challenge was that this dentist was fifty miles away.

Wes and I loaded David and Zack into the car and headed for the dental offices forty-five minutes away. Wes' name was called and I sat in the small waiting room with a bored toddler and a restless baby. I decided to take the boys for a walk so I asked the receptionist how long Wes' appointment would be. She told me to return in about an hour and a half. That seemed to be a long time to just treat one tooth.

When I returned to the dentist's office, Wes was still not in the waiting room. I asked the nurse where he was and she said, "I'll get him for you."

The door opened and the nurse wheeled out a semi-conscious Wes. He had undergone extensive oral surgery and was still heavily sedated.

It was then I realized my predicament: I was holding the hand of my three year old, David, I had four month old Zachary in the stroller, Wes in a wheelchair and I was forty-five minutes away from someone's house in a country I had only been in for two weeks.

Fortunately, I had paid attention on the drive to the dentist's surgery so I had a vague recollection of how to get back to the house where we were staying. I prayed fervently as I maneuvered my way onto the freeway. It was only the second time I had driven on a freeway and the last time, my husband had been coherent!

With all three boys sleeping soundly in the car, I gripped the steering wheel, and though I was still getting used to driving on the opposite side of the road with the steering wheel on the left instead of the right, I headed for the freeway. While driving, I thanked God for every small victory. I praised God for successfully finding my way to the freeway. I praised God that I remembered which freeway exit to take, and praised God at each intersection. I kept myself securely covered in a garment of praise.

I finally reached our friends' house and brought Zachary safely inside under the watchful eye of his big brother, then I helped Wes upstairs so he could sleep off the effects of the sedation. I sat down on the sofa and just breathed a grateful prayer of thanks to God for His guidance and protection. In the midst of difficult and challenging circumstances, I had experienced the joy of knowing God's presence was with me.

The apostle, Paul, knew the value of praising God despite his circumstances. While imprisoned, Paul wrote these words: "Rejoice in the Lord always. I will say it again: Rejoice!" (Philippians 4:4) As author Cathy Lechner says, "You can't rejoice unless you first 'joice'!"[2]

In other words, we need to praise God first, and then again, and again.

We need to be joyful in all things, even when it feels as if we have little reason to rejoice. Look for things for which we can praise God. Be intentional about praising God. Even though he was in prison, Paul was strongly living out his message to "Rejoice in the Lord always." Yes, always.

4

Find the Fun

Joy is strength— Joy is love— Joy is a net of
love by which you can catch souls.
Mother Teresa

Here are two words that should never be in one
sentence: mandatory and meeting. I don't mind attending meetings but something happens to my attitude
when it is mandatory.

One evening, I was preparing to attend one such
meeting. My friend, Angie, called and I complained
that my evening was going to be lost to a mandatory
meeting. Angie, repeating the words she has said on
many occasions before this one, said, "Ellie, just find
the fun."

JOY!

There have been a number of times when Angie and I have said these words to one another. We seem to find the fun in most situations. We have found the fun as we traveled eighteen hundred miles to Iowa with five kids in the car. We have found the fun as we changed a flat tire on the side of a suburban road after a visit to the hair salon. If there is one thing we can do, it is to turn most situations into fun.

On a trip to the East Coast, one of our flights was cancelled and we had to be re-routed through another airport. When we finally reached our destination, we discovered our luggage did not keep up with our changed flights. We were in Virginia, and our luggage was in North Carolina.

Rather than complain about the situation, Angie and I chose a different approach. We checked into our hotel and told the receptionist that, hopefully, our luggage would be sent there before midnight. Since we had so much time on our hands, we asked her, "Where's the nearest mall?"

We figured we might as well enjoy the day. Despite the lack of sleep and the uncertainty of the fate of our luggage, we had fun exploring a mall and imagining what things we would need to buy if our luggage was never found!

But how could I find the fun in a meeting attended by other people whose attendance was, like me, under duress? With Angie's challenge in mind, I was determined to find the fun in what was proving to be an uninspiring meeting. I knew that she would ask me if anything fun had emerged from the meeting. It wasn't looking good.

One of the women attending that meeting had recently been through a heartbreaking period in her life. During the coffee break, I decided to push aside my 'poor me' attitude and sought to befriend her. I introduced myself to her and then spent the next forty-five minutes listening to this mother as she shared her sorrow.

As I drove home that evening, I noticed that my complaining attitude had been replaced with a heart of compassion for someone else. I drove home with a heart of gratitude for the health of my husband and my sons.

The evening had proved to be worthwhile and I had found the fun in an unlikely situation. But this kind of fun was found only when I overcame my selfishness and sought to help someone else. I had been reminded of one of the keys to joy.

Be Third

One of the earliest teachings that I recall from my years in Sunday School was to put the needs of others first. Maybe it was such a memorable teaching because it was so practical. Even as a seven year old, I knew that I should look for ways to help others whether it was my neighbor, my friends, even, and perhaps more difficult, my sisters.

I remember, too, the simple song that reinforced this teaching:

> J-o-y, j-o-y
> This must surely be
> Jesus first and myself last
> And others in between.

In this simple song, joy is an acronym for Jesus, others, then you. The acronym may be easy to remember, but it is often difficult to live. However, if we want to preserve and nurture our joy, we need to keep that order of priorities in our life.

I'm not a big fan of televised sports. I will watch a basketball game and I love the Olympic games. But I have no desire to watch any other sports, especially football. I don't understand American football. I am unable to name ten football teams. But I love the life philosophy of Hall of Famer and Chicago Bears (1965-1971) running back, Gale Sayers.

Gale Sayers titled his autobiography, *I Am Third*, because as he says, "the Lord is first; my family and friends are second; I am third."[1] I may not know what a running back does but I know Gale Sayers has discovered one of the keys to a joyful life.

Too often, we mistakenly believe that the way to experience joy is to look after our own interests and our own needs. Spend too long on this quest, and you will discover that this road never leads to joy. A life spent in selfish pursuits is unsatisfying, unrewarding and not the kind of life God intended for us.

Jesus spent his life in service to others. Far from pursuing his own agenda, the Bible tells us "for the joy set before him endured the cross" (Hebrews 12:2). Imagine that. Jesus was able to endure his suffering because he was focusing on helping us. He went to the cross with joy because he was rescuing a fallen people.

There is an incredible joy that emerges within us when we serve others. It is deep and satisfying.

Two years ago, I was part of a mission's team that traveled to Europe to provide childcare for the children of missionaries who were attending a conference. Prior to the conference, I spent five days in Switzerland with a group from the childcare team. We stayed in a chalet with a view of Jungfrau, one of the largest mountains in the Swiss Alps. It was breathtakingly beautiful. One day, we hiked in the Alps. It was like a scene from *The Sound of Music*. I kept looking for Julie Andrews amidst the mountain goats.

The next week was spent in a conference center. It coincided with one of the worst heat waves in Europe's history. It was a far cry from the picturesque chalet in Switzerland! I worked nine or ten hours a day looking after twenty, often unsettled, two year olds.

The work was challenging and the days were long. And yet, I experienced such joy. The parents of these children are missionaries in some of the most difficult countries of the world. In caring for these little ones, I felt like I was serving people who gave selflessly to God's work. Being third was a richly rewarding and joyful experience.

Serve with Gladness

In the King James version of the Bible, Psalm 100:5 says, "Serve the Lord with gladness." It is one thing to seek ways to serve God, it is another to do it with a heart of gladness or joy. As we give ourselves in service to others, we can easily feel drained and weary. In these conditions, our joy can be depleted and what we are left with is a begrudging spirit, serving not with gladness, but with frustration and resentment.

Jesus modeled a life of service. He continually gave his time and energy to people. Wherever Jesus went there were people wanting him to perform a miracle, to heal them or to teach them. His days were spent giving himself to the needs of others. It must have been exhausting! How did Jesus keep his joy when his days were so full of tending to the needs of others?

In Matthew 14:23, it says, "After Jesus dismissed them [the crowd], he went up on a mountainside by himself to pray." In Mark 5:16, we read: "But Jesus often withdrew to lonely places to pray." Jesus knew that in order to keep his joy in such draining and exhausting conditions, he needed to find time so He could re-connect with God, His father. He needed periods of rest and renewal.

There were so many people needing Jesus' attention and his touch. Likewise, we may find ourselves with many people requiring our attention and our help. Yet, Jesus knew in order to be effective in the long term, he needed to withdraw to places of quiet prayer.

JOY!

In order to keep a heart of gladness as we serve, we need to carve out time for quiet; time for re-connecting with our Heavenly Father. Being third means that others' needs may come before our own, but our priority is to keep God in first position.

God does not intend for us to do it all in our own strength. We need times with Him for rest and renewal. This will preserve our gladness as we serve. We will keep our joy.

5

A changed perspective

Joy springs from a life lived with
eternity's values in view.
Chuck Swindoll

If there is one thing that continues to amaze me
about living in Southern California, it is the traffic.
Any time, day or night, there is lots of it. It seems
there is no such thing as a deserted freeway.

The freeways of Los Angeles have a formidable repu-
tation. Even when I lived in Australia, I had heard of
the infamous freeways. I had heard sometimes people
even get shot on these freeways. On my first visit to
LA, I had a memorable freeway experience.

JOY!

Wes and I had come to Southern California for a vacation. We had arranged to stay in the home of a wonderful couple who were in their late sixties. The husband had kindly agreed to pick us up from Los Angeles International airport and take us to his home in Anaheim. Naively, we had booked a flight that would arrive at five o'clock, right in the middle of rush hour.

I had never seen so many cars in one place, at one time. I had never seen a freeway that had ten lanes across with traffic moving in both directions. Did I write moving? Crawling is a more apt description. As I was processing all the sights, I noticed something else: the gentleman who was driving us to his home was an erratic driver.

As the traffic moved forward, he would suddenly accelerate then he would slam on his brakes hard to avoid colliding with the car in front. The car would come to a halting stop. He would then accelerate again, and then he would stop. Accelerate. Stop. Accelerate. Stop.

We did that for an hour and a half. I spent the time praying that he would not hit the car in front, that the driver in front did not have a gun, and that I would not throw up in the back seat of this man's car.

A Changed Perspective

The freeways in Southern California are an efficient way of moving traffic from one county to the next county. However, the high volume of traffic on the freeways means that it does not take much to reduce the speed of the moving traffic to a grinding halt. If a minor fender bender occurs in one lane, then the flow of traffic in the other lanes is reduced to a frustrating crawl.

Now that I am a seasoned traveler on these freeways, I've become adept at dealing with the nuances and challenges of freeway congestion. What I find most frustrating is when the freeway slows to a crawl and there is no logical explanation for the delay.

My frustration at being in a situation that is outside of my control is intensified because I don't know what is the best course of action: Should I stay on the freeway? What is causing the delay? Is the traffic ahead moving? How long will the delay last? Should I take the next exit? Where does the exit lead?

The best source of answers for these questions, I have discovered, is to tune into specific radio stations that provide frequent and up-to-the-minute traffic reports. Of course, who provides the information for these traffic reports? The helicopter circling overhead. From that vantage point, the news reporter on board the helicopter can view the situation and provide information about the delays, the detours and the best alternate routes.

There are times when we are traveling along a certain path and we encounter an unexpected delay. I'm not talking about traffic and freeways here, but life. A road-block slows our progress and we immediately wonder what to do and how long the delay will last. That which we were once so sure of is suddenly uncertain.

We may suddenly find ourselves in a situation where we are no longer in control. This can give rise to much frustration, impatience, and uncertainty which can overshadow our joy.

In those times, we need a changed perspective. We need to trust in the One whose vantage point provides a clear picture of what is happening. Like a helicopter hovering over a grid locked freeway, God sees what you cannot.

God sees the road ahead, and, if you continue to trust in Him, He will lead you in the way you should go. As it says in Isaiah 30:21:

> "Whether you turn to the right or to the left, your ears will hear a voice behind you saying, 'This is the way; walk in it.'"

Straight Paths

My perspective on life is so limited. What I see is clouded by my desires, my emotions and my, often-times, flawed thinking. That is why I treasure the words from Proverbs 3:5-6:

> "Trust in the Lord with all your heart and
> lean not on your own understanding; in all
> your ways acknowledge him and he will
> make your paths straight."

These words are a reminder that whatever situation we may face, we need to trust in God wholeheartedly.

Rather than leaning on my understanding of a situation, I need to lean on the One who sees it all: my past, my present and my future. I have discovered that it is usually with the benefit of hindsight that life makes sense and that as I look back on my life, I can see how God has been constantly directing my path.

Before making the move from living in Australia to live in the United States, God had been straightening my path to lead me through this huge transition. Until then, I had always prided myself (yes, pride was definitely involved) on being a working mother. It seemed that with good planning, it was possible to juggle motherhood and career. In fact, I could not imagine choosing anything else.

When I was pregnant with David, I completed my Master's degree. It seemed a good move as it would open the door to future opportunities in the field of education, which would allow me to work part-time and raise my children.

After David was born, I returned to teaching part-time as planned. But when I had a miscarriage in 1993, I decided it would be a good time to return to full-time teaching. My passion was for teaching. I loved the school community and was looking forward to increasing my teaching hours.

The school board where I worked had been in the process of incorporating a small, struggling Christian school into their administrative structure. They needed someone who would be willing to take on the role as head teacher at this school which was twenty miles away. I was given the position.

What I thought was going to be a good career move was in reality a difficult and at times, heartbreaking experience. I went from being the popular teacher of one school to being viewed as a representative of the hostile take-over. The existing teaching staff, two women who were best friends, did not welcome me.

My authority was questioned, my abilities were doubted and in time, my biggest critic was myself.

I was given a combination fourth, fifth and sixth grade class to teach while trying to raise the school's profile in the community and deal with the day to day running of a school. At the same time, Wes' ministry required him to be absent for long stretches of time as he traveled around Australia and to the United States. The highlight of my day was picking up David from childcare. At least, he still liked me.

What I had considered to be a good, well-planned path for my life was being diverted in another direction. My love for teaching was being eroded. My hard work to overcome a challenging work situation seemed to be achieving little. My quest to prove my value to this school was tainted by my announcement that I was pregnant and would not see out the school year.

It was during those months that Wes decided to reapply for a worker's visa for entry into the United States. Despite being unsuccessful on a previous attempt, this time his application was accepted. Wes visited me at work to share his news.

A move to the United States was something Wes had always talked about doing one day. It seemed that day had arrived. I was going to move away from my family and friends with a toddler and a new baby. And for the first time in my life, I had no career plan. The requirement of our visa entry was that I would be unable to work for the next three to five years.

I vividly remember the day we left Australia. There is a photo of us walking through the departure gates at Sydney airport: David, with an oversized koala back-pack, four month old Zachary in my arms and Wes, grinning in anticipation of this big adventure.

My career plans were shelved and I discovered myself on a path never considered: I was a stay-at-home mom. I was on the other side of the planet from my family and friends and I was at home all day, everyday, with two small children. All the while, Wes was throwing himself into transferring his ministry from Australia to America. From my perspective, I had stalled on the road. Although I could not see where this path was leading, I had to trust in God.

The more I trusted in Him and leaned on Him, I could see He was straightening my path. God led me along a road where I was no longer able to make the plans for my life. Instead, I had to depend on Him for each uncertain step.

No longer able to rest on my confidence as a success-ful woman managing her career and children, I had to find my confidence in Him. My value had to be found in obeying God even if that meant forgoing my plans and supporting my husband as he traveled and developed his ministry.

I felt as if I was stalled on that road for a long time. Yet all the while, God was allowing me to grow in my understanding of His goodness and provision.

My love of teaching I began to invest into the lives of David and Zachary as I discovered I could homeschool them. We were able to travel as a family, we had wonderful times with family and friends from Australia who visited us (after all, we are just thirty minutes from Disneyland), and Wes and I began to work alongside one another encouraging other people to experience an abundant life.

God led me along the path to a life better than I could ever have planned. I had no idea God had so much in store for me!

Gracia Burnham and her husband, Martin, were missionaries in the Philippines. In May 2001, they were kidnapped by a Muslim extremist group and were held as hostages for over twelve months. As they were finally being rescued, Martin Burnham was killed in the gun battle between the rescuers and the kidnappers.

In her book, *To Fly Again*, Gracia shares how she has sought to overcome the challenges and to rebuild her life since the tragic loss of her husband. In describing her journey, Gracia writes:

> "At times it is hard to see cause for joy in our life. When our circumstances have conspired to wear us down, to drain our patience, to dash our hopes and dreams, we feel within us the very opposite of joy. We are frustrated and, even sometimes resentful.
> Only the long perspective, the divine perspective can bring back the joy to our heart. Only when we remind ourselves that 'God is for us' (Romans 8:31) never against us, can we rise above our immediate feelings."[1]

In those times when we experience an unexpected delay or detour, we need to change from our limited perspective to consider that God has a different vantage point and He can see the road ahead.

Your joy can too easily be hidden by the burden of uncertainty and impatience. In those times, strengthen your joy by leaning on God and get ready to see where He is leading you.

In this way, you'll be like the person described by the Psalmist— the object of God's delight because he

A Changed Perspective

"walks in step with God; his path blazed by God, he's happy. If he stumbles, he's not down for long; God has a grip on his hand" (Psalm 37:23 The Message).

Look Up!

. . . the people of God ought to be the happiest
people in all the wide world! People should be
coming to us constantly and asking the source
of our joy and delight.
A. W. Tozer

My friend, Jo, is a triathlete. She is energetic and
inspiring. Her enthusiasm is contagious. Of course,
knowing that, I really should have kept clear of her lest
I catch her enthusiasm for athletic pursuits. Too late.

A few years ago, Jo encouraged me to enter a
triathlon as part of a relay team. I love to swim and Jo
assured me that all I had to do was swim the equivalent

of ten laps of an Olympic sized pool. Of course, it wasn't a pool. It was a lake. It was a cold, murky lake full of swimmers with thrashing arms and legs trying to reach the other side. It was so much fun!

Next, Jo convinced me that if I could ride a bike and run a few miles, then I could complete a short distance triathlon. Riding a bike would be easy but running has never been my thing. Not a problem, Jo assured me, a brisk walk would suffice. That summer, I completed two short distance triathlons: I swam, I biked and predominately walked my way to the finish line.

As much as I would have been content with my accomplishments, Jo was ready with a new challenge. Last year, she completed a marathon in San Francisco. She raved enthusiastically about her experience and convinced me this was something I needed to do.

So I am currently training for a half marathon. I have been running for the past two years and I have participated in a few 5K races just for fun. With Jo alongside enthusiastically cheering me on, I may just make that half marathon.

One thing I have discovered in training runs is that watching the path is never inspiring. When I have my eyes focused on the ground, I am likely to notice every slow moving step. I am more inclined to notice my aches and pains. And thoughts of quitting come to mind. It is then I remind myself to look up. With my eyes looking up, I can enjoy my surroundings, I can set my sights on the road ahead, and look out for the finish line.

In those times when my eyes are down, my vision is limited to what is immediately before me. No wonder Paul advises us to "set your minds on things above" (Colossians 3:2). *The Message* says it this way:

> "Don't shuffle along, eyes on the ground, absorbed with the things right in front of you. Look up and be alert to what is going on around Christ— that is where the action is. See things from his perspective."

What a good description! With our eyes on the ground, we become absorbed in what is directly in front of us. When I run with my eyes down, all I see is the uninspiring and monotonous path. It is this monotony that can change a run from being enjoyable to tedious.

So, too, the path of life can be tedious. If we don't lift our eyes, all we see are the same things over and over. It is the tedious, day in and day out tasks that can, if we are not careful, drain our joy.

JOY!

In the Everyday

After David was born, I was often asked, "Are you planning to return to teaching?" My response was always, "Absolutely!" I couldn't imagine staying home with a baby. I knew there would be plenty to do; it was just that the type of work did not inspire me. As columnist Erma Bombeck once wrote: "Housework is a treadmill from futility to oblivion with stop offs at tedium and counter productivity." I couldn't have agreed more.

When we moved to the United States, I became a stay-at-home mom. We had limited financial resources, one vehicle and I had yet to make any friends. My days were spent keeping house and caring for a toddler and a baby. With not much else to fill my days, I even considered making handicrafts. Fortunately, that thought passed since my skills in this area are very limited!

Paul Thigpen in his article titled, *Where's the Joy?* writes, "Sometimes joy seems to elude us most in the everyday routine. The world seems gray; the hours are endless. We aren't particularly distressed, but we don't find much pleasure in what we do."[1] He suggests that just as when things are not going well, it is in the every-day that we need to "catch a glimpse of the Lord."[2]

In times of crisis or hardship, our desperation causes us to cry out to God for His comfort, His strength and His peace. We desperately seek God. It is in these times of going through the fire, that our faith is refined. We nail our colors to the mast and declare that we will not be swayed. It is a time when trusting in God is essential to survival.

Yet, it is in the everyday drudgery of life that we have to be even more determined to keep seeking God. We need to keep our faith forging forward. Oswald Chambers says,

> "Drudgery is one of the finest touchstones of character there is. Drudgery is work that is far removed from anything to do with the ideal— the utterly mean, grubbing things; and when we come in contact with them we know instantly whether or not we are spiritually real."[3]

Washing the dishes, cleaning the bathroom, paying the bills, changing diapers, and making macaroni and cheese (again!), are tasks that could be considered drudgery. In those humdrum periods, we need to look up and remind ourselves that we are in the process of becoming more patient, more gracious, something more like Jesus. In this way, we can make these tasks less like drudgery and more like something divine.

The tedium of chores and the less than stimulating conversation with my boys when they were little, could have sapped my joy. If I had kept looking only at the path immediately in front of me, the drudgery could have dehydrated the flow of joy. With my eyes downcast, my joy would have been depleted.

Instead, I had to do what it says in Psalm 121:

> "I lift up my eyes to the hills— where does my help come from? My help comes from the Lord, the Maker of heaven and earth." (Psalm 121:1-2)

This verse reminded me then, and it still reminds me today, to look up and look to the presence of the Maker of heaven and earth.

To survive that season of my life, I required the help that comes from God. As foolish as it seems, I would pray as I unloaded the dishwasher. I would ask God for His strength as I dealt with a two year old's temper tantrum. I would ask God for His peace as I faced a house that had been upended by two energetic boys.

Most nights (if I hadn't already fallen asleep) I would ask God to help me enjoy my situation and to savor every day with David and Zachary.

Look Up!

In the book, *The Practice of the Presence of God*, Brother Lawrence, a monk who lived in the seventeenth century, says:

> "that we should not be weary of doing little things for the love of God who looks not at the grandeur of these actions but rather at the love with which they are performed; that we should not be surprised at failing often in the beginning but that in the end we will acquire a habit which will allow us to perform our acts effortlessly and with great pleasure."[4]

According to Brother Lawrence, it is in the little things, maybe even the mundane, that we can express our love for God. As we look to God in the drudgery of the everyday, we will feel a release from the effort, and experience joy.

I am so thankful for the lessons that I learned during those years when the boys were little. I look back on those years as being a happy time. I discovered the joy of being at home and had the privilege of spending a lot of time with David and Zachary. In fact, by the time my immigration status was upgraded and I was able to work again, I chose to continue to stay at home.

My days are still filled with those same mundane

tasks. Because David and Zachary are at home all day, and because Wes and I work from home, our house is constantly full of people. This means there is rarely a stretch of time when I can get the house clean and it stays that way. The kitchen countertops, the floors and the bathrooms are constantly in need of my attention.

Most days, I can usually keep my joy in the midst of the humdrum. If you ever stop by unannounced, and I am complaining, remind me to lift my eyes and see not the drudgery, but the divine.

7

Enjoy the Ride

Grief can take care of itself, but to get
the full value of a joy you must have
somebody to divide it with.
Mark Twain

When I was growing up, my parents could not afford to take the family to theme parks. So I had my first experience of a roller coaster ride when I was seventeen years old. That summer, a carnival came to the town where we were vacationing and there was a roller coaster.

Now compared to today's roller coasters this was not particularly impressive. It seemed not too intimidating.

So I convinced my younger sister, Annie, to ride the coaster with me. What a ride!

This coaster consisted of little cars that traveled at fast speeds along a track. The turns were sharp. So sharp, it looked as if the car was going to fly off the track until, with an abrupt turn, the car righted itself and followed the track. There were dips, turns, more dips, and more abrupt turns. I was suddenly aware that Annie was not having fun. Her head was burrowed in my back and she was muttering something about wanting to get off.

I have since tried to convince her that her coaster experience has been tainted. I'm sure with a trip to Disneyland, I could introduce her to a whole new side of thrill rides. I'm looking forward to that day.

A few years ago, my other sister, Sue, visited me and we took a trip to California Adventure, Disneyland's other theme park in Anaheim. Sue's sons, Addison and Jack, along with David and Zachary, convinced Sue and me that we should ride the California Screamin' coaster. Our reputations as 'cool moms' was on the line. We agreed to ride the roller coaster with the boys.

This roller coaster was bigger and faster than the one I had ridden with Annie. It took off at an alarming speed, made a loop, had a huge drop (the perfect photo opportunity), and many twists and turns. I treasure the photo of Sue and me from that ride. It captures our enjoyment as is evident in our wide-mouthed grins.

Many times, our lives feel like roller coaster rides. The sudden drops, the exhilarating turns and the constant motion of our lives can make for terrifying rides. On the other hand, it can make for a lot of laughter.

One thing is for certain; it is always better to have someone to share in the ride. Whether it is to grip their hand in terror, or to share in the excitement, it is much better with someone by your side.

Of course, the right traveling companions will impact how much you enjoy the ride. Choose the wrong companion and your joy may diminish. The right companion or friend and your joy will increase.

Friends that Bring Joy

The Bible has much to say about the topic of friendship. One of my favorite proverbs says, "A righteous man is cautious in friendship" (Proverbs 12:26). It is important to act with caution as you add new friends to your life. It is important to have friendships that build not burden you; friendships that are constructive not destructive; friendships that energize you not drain you.

The best friendships are those which evolve gradually over time. Being cautious means not rushing to build a new friendship with phone calls, shared meals and big investments of time until you have discerned the quality of the person's character. As it says in 1 Corinthians 15:33: "Do not be misled: bad company corrupts good character." Look for the qualities of good character like honesty, respect, and reliability. Don't make friends with someone who gossips: if they are gossiping about their last friend, it is just a matter of time before they are gossiping to someone about you.

I heard evangelist, Jesse Duplantis, once say: "I am wary of anyone who does not have old friends." In other words, be careful of the person who is rapidly building new friendship in the wake of discarded relationships. If someone can not keep a friend for more than a fleeting season, the chances are they will not be a faithful friend to you.

Finding good friends can add so much to your life. They have the power to speak into your life, to build you up and to hold your hand when the ride of life gets a little terrifying. As author Edna Buchanan states: "Friends are the family you choose for yourself."

Wise Friends

Maureen is wonderful friend. She is an amazing mother of four children, a pastor's wife and worship leader. Maureen is a faithful and caring friend. Like me, she loves coffee, the beach and music.

Yet what I value most in Maureen is that she is wise. Now being called wise can bring to mind images of someone who wears sensible shoes and has her hair pulled back in a tight bun. But Maureen is far from that picture. She is a living example that wisdom and style are not mutually exclusive!

Maureen is wise because she knows the One who is the source of wisdom. She knows "the fear of the Lord" which is the beginning of wisdom (Proverbs 1:7). She has the ability to navigate her way through the challenges of life. No matter the changing tides or the storms, she stays afloat because she stays close to God.

In Proverbs 13:20, it says: "He who walks with the wise grows wise, but a companion of fools suffers harm." In other words, we become like those with whom we spend time.

If you value wisdom, then build relationships with wise people. Seek out these relationships. When I first spent time with Maureen, she spoke of her relationship with Jesus with such enthusiasm and vitality, that I found I wanted to be like her. Her passion for God and her joy were infectious.

As it turned out, we had lots in common. We were both married to pastors, we were living away from our families, we were homeschooling our children, and we were the same age. (Although Maureen would quickly remind me that I am six months older than her!)

In the years when we lived in the same town, Maureen and I would get together once a week for an early morning game of tennis, coffee and Bible study. She ignited in me a renewed love for God's Word. She introduced me to good books and constantly modeled how to be a godly mother.

Through my friendship with Maureen, I have gained a greater understanding of living life with the wisdom that comes from God. This friendship has brought such joy to my life. Life has brought its fair share of unexpected turns and dramatic drops, but like a roller coaster ride, it has been much more fun to experience it together.

Close Friends

I have been blessed with a wonderful family. I love my parents, dearly. I have two lovely sisters, Sue and Annie, and one amazing brother, Robert, with whom I never seem to spend enough time. Of course, they all live in Australia and there is often a year or more between visits. My times with them are precious.

Missing my family has been a constant challenge since living in America. While there is the telephone and e-mail, there is nothing like being able to celebrate holidays and birthdays together, and being a part of one another's lives. I lament that my children are missing out on being with their grandparents, uncles and aunts, and cousins.

If I were to dwell on what I am missing and focus on my losses, my joy could so easily be extinguished. Instead, I need to rejoice for what I have been given.

And I have been given a lot. In the absence of my extended family, I have been given friendships that are like family. In Proverbs 18:24 it says: "A man of many companions may come to ruin, but there is a friend who sticks closer than a brother."

In other words, rather than trying to balance many

relationships with companions, which may be superficial and not beneficial, develop relationships with those friends who become like family.

I have many friends who have added so much to my life. I continue to enjoy friendships that were formed in grade school. I continue to invest in many of my friends in Australia. Yet being in America, without family, I have found friends who stick closer than a brother or sister.

I like the wisdom of Proverbs 27:10 as found in *The Message*. It says:

> "Do not leave your friends or your parents' friends and run home to your family when things get rough; Better a nearby friend than a distant family."

Angie's family lives in Iowa, my family lives in Australia and so, we have become like family. She is like a sister. We share fun times, we support each other when it is 'one of those days', and we can talk and laugh for hours. Considering I look nothing like her and I have an Australian accent, it is always surprising when people ask if we are sisters. Angie is family not by birth, but by choice.

I meet many people who because of work or finances, have to live far away from their families.

Thankfully, we can still keep in contact with our families. We can e-mail photos, we can talk on the phone, and we can send text messages. There are many things we can do to lessen the feelings of being apart.

But don't overlook the value of a close friend. When family is distant, enjoy the friend who is nearby. Life shared with a good friend will bring much joy to the ride of life.

8

No Place I'd Rather Be

Cheerfulness keeps up a kind of daylight in the
mind, and fills it with a steady and perpetual serenity.
Joseph Addison (1672-1719)

I heard this joke recently: How many country music
stars does it take to change a light bulb? Three: One to
change the light bulb, and two to sing about it. I love
that joke because it points to the unique ability of
country music to produce songs about everyday things.
Not that I am an expert on country music. I am,
thanks to Angie's influence, learning to appreciate this
genre of music.

One country song I do like is Phil Vassar's song, *Just
Another Day in Paradise*. The song describes a typical

scenario in so many homes with "the kids screaming, phone ringing, the dog's barking at the mailman bringing that stack of bills— overdue."[1] After painting a picture of household chaos, Phil Vassar sings that he "thanks the Lord for just another day in paradise."

I wonder if, like Phil Vassar, you refer to the mayhem in your home as another day in paradise. I know paradise isn't a word that immediately comes to my mind. But I do agree with Phil Vassar's sentiment when he says, "there's no place I'd rather be." I may be away from my family, I may still be a stay-at-home mom, I may be living in a country where everyone drives on the opposite side of the road and where it is winter when it should be summer and vice versa, but there is no other place I'd rather be.

A friend of mine, Beth, does not feel that way. She has had to be re-located because of her husband's work — not an uncommon scenario these days. Beth, and her young family, had to move to New Mexico. Her parents and friends were in her hometown in California.

Despite being able to return to visit her family for an annual vacation, she has spent the past seven years living in New Mexico. Two of her children were born there and yet, she has longed for the day when her husband's work would allow them to return to her home state.

Recently, Beth received word that they would be returning to California. I expected that she would be elated. No, she is lamenting that she has to re-locate. After seven years of being less than content with her situation, she is uncertain the move is going to be good for her family and is anxious about the transition.

When we arrived in California, I made a determined effort to enjoy this experience. At the time, Wes and I anticipated that we would be in the country for just five years so I was going to make the most of this time.

In Australia, I had enjoyed being a part of choirs and vocal groups, so I decided that I would join the church choir. I had been in the country just a few weeks and I drove myself, an accomplishment in those early days, to the church and found the room where I could hear the choir rehearsing. It turned out that rehearsal started at 7:00 p.m., not at 7:30 p.m. as I expected. In Australia, evening meetings often start on the half hour as do television programs. Choir rehearsal was already underway.

It would have been so easy to turn and head back home. Instead, I took a deep breath and walked into the rehearsal apologizing for my tardiness. I met some people in the alto section and agreed to be there for choir performances on the next Sunday.

This may not seem significant but it took an effort to resist the urge to stay at home. I could have resisted building relationships with people thinking that I was only going to be in the country for a few years. But I knew that the way to enjoy this period of transition was to meet new friends and feel a sense of belonging, even if it was just a church choir.

Over the next twelve months, I continued my quest to enjoy my life here. Wes and I purchased family passes for Disneyland. I scouted out the best malls. I found the best places for coffee and at the park, I would point out every squirrel (a novelty to an Aussie) to David and Zachary. By the time my parents made a visit to the States, we had so much we wanted to share with them. They could see that even though I was far from home, I was content.

choose contentment

Mind you, there are still days when I can lose myself in complaints about my lot. I can become discontent with being so far from my family. I can regret that my sons do not spend much time with their cousins. But I have learned that the end result of making an effort to enjoy my current circumstances brings contentment, and that contentment produces joy. As we are encouraged in Hebrews 13:5, "be content with what you have."

And we do have so much. Yet, feelings of discontent can easily develop and conceal our joy. A sense of dissatisfaction can creep into our life and, in time, our joy is hidden under the debris of discontent.

When we become discontent, we fail to see the blessings God has given. We cease to consider what we have received and harbor feelings of envy and dissatisfaction. These are not conducive to joy. Mark Reed in his article, *Choosing Joy*, states, "When we worry over the things we don't have, instead of finding contentment in what we do have, joy shrivels and dies."[2]

We need to remember that the purpose of most advertising is to cause us to feel discontent. How else can they convince us that we need to have their product? Advertisers plant a seed of discontent so that we will purchase their product. Of course, it is just a matter of time before we are no longer content with that new house, new car, new shoes, or new whatever.

I was an avid reader of fashion magazines. I loved to see the latest trends, to read about the new products and to critique the 'what not to wear' section. But I began to notice how, after reading a magazine, I became dissatisfied with my own life, my own home, and the way I look. I became discontent.

I have since given up my subscriptions to fashion magazines. In fact, the only magazine I subscribe to now is *Discipleship Journal*. The articles encourage me to seek God and to grow in my faith. Now, if they could just include a column of upcoming fashion trends, it would be perfect!

How often do we fail to enjoy what we have because it's not what we think we want? Too often, we can let our joy diminish simply because we fail to see what we have been given, or what blessings God has provided. It is a little bit of the 'I'll be happy when. . .' syndrome that so easily creeps into life. You know, 'I'll be happy when I get that promotion,' 'I'll be happy when I get a bigger home,' or 'I'll be happy when the kids grow out of this stage.'

In Psalm 118:24, it says: "This is the day that the Lord has made; I will rejoice and be glad in it." As Joel Osteen writes in his book, *Your Best Life Now*:

"Notice he [the writer of the psalm] didn't say, 'Tomorrow I will be happy.' He didn't say, 'Next week, when I don't have so many problems, I'm going to rejoice.' No, he said,

'This is the day.' This is the day that God wants me to be happy."[3]

We need to experience joy today. Celebrate this day. Otherwise, we will miss the moments of today that are worth celebrating and rejoicing in because we are longing for something else.

Contentment is a means to securing our joy. It causes us to cover our frustrations and dissatisfaction with the garment of praise. Rather than becoming a target for Satan's attack, we can "resist the devil and he will flee" (James 4:7). Rather than being weak and vulnerable, we can hold firm to the strength that is founded in our joy.

Paul, the Apostle, knew about contentment. Writing from his prison cell which I expect was hardly a fun part of town, Paul says:

> "I'm just as happy with little as with much, with much as with little. . . whatever I have, wherever I am, I can make it through in the One who makes me who I am." (Philippians 4:11-13 The Message)

Despite his joyless circumstances, Paul knew that the key to maintaining his joy was to be content with "whatever I have" and "wherever I am."

JOY!

Take a look at your surroundings and circumstances and thank God for all you have been given. Praise God for His goodness. In time, your surroundings may not feel quite like paradise but you will begin to experience the kind of contentment Paul described. You may even feel as if there's no place you'd rather be.

9

uniquely You

Joy comes from seeing the complete fulfillment of
the specific purpose for which I was created and
born again, not from successfully doing
something of my own choosing.
Oswald Chambers

Being content with our circumstances is one thing;
being content with who we are is a whole different
challenge. If I spend time comparing myself with
someone else or wishing I look a certain way or possessed
certain gifts and abilities, my joy will rapidly drain
away. In time, I will be no longer content or thankful
for God's many blessings.

JOY!

Stacey S. Padrick in her article, *Invasion of the Joy Snatchers* writes:

> "Discontent and ungratefulness are like two greedy hands pulling the stopper in our bathtub of joy. When we focus upon our lack in relation to another's lot (larger home, more clients, better looks, stronger health), we are silently saying to God, 'Why didn't you give me what You gave him? Why haven't you been as good to me as her?' We question God's goodness, faithfulness, and love."[1]

That was certainly the experience of King Saul, the first king of Israel. He had been handpicked by God to lead His beloved nation of Israel. He is described in the Bible as "an impressive young man without equal among the Israelites— a head taller than any of the others" (1 Samuel 9:2). King Saul had the potential to lead courageously but he failed to obey God and was swayed by his own desires.

While Saul was king, young David killed the giant, Goliath, who had been intimidating the armies of Israel. When David returned home, there was much celebrating with dancing in the streets. The women sang, "Saul has slain his thousands, David has slain his tens of thousands" (1 Samuel 18:7). Ouch, what a comparison!

King Saul's response to this was anger. Rather than acknowledging all that God had bestowed upon him, Saul was envious. The Bible says "And from that time on Saul kept a jealous eye on David" (1 Samuel 18:9).

With one eye on David, Saul was constantly restless, watching David's actions and fretting about his future. From this time on, the Bible records King Saul's downward spiral to insanity.

Comparing myself with others is a sure way to drive myself crazy. In Ephesians 4:27, Paul warns us to "not give the devil a foothold." When I begin comparing myself with others, it is like unlocking the door and extending an invitation to the thief who comes to "kill, steal and destroy." It is like handing over my joy and giving away my strength.

When I start comparing myself with someone else, it is as if I disregard how God has made me. It is effectively saying to God, 'I don't want to be the way I am; I want to be the same as that person.' Reflecting on this desire in people to be like one another, Pastor Paul de Jong challenges, "If you want to make a difference, be different."

Embrace the Pink

Last winter, pink was the new fashion favorite. There were pink bags, pink shoes, pink everything. I am not a big fan of the color pink. It may look fantastic on some. I think it makes me look washed out.

One day, as Angie and I were in the mall, we were confronted by rows of pink shirts. That day, Angie, sensing my less than enthusiastic attitude, challenged me with these words: "Embrace the pink."

Sometimes, there is something about ourselves we just don't like. We may apologize for the color of our hair or skin. We may be embarrassed by our height, or by the size of our thighs. We may regret our lack of culinary skills (that's mine!) or our lack of athletic or technical ability. We may downplay these inadequacies or try to disguise our faults (that's why they invented cover-ups for the beach). Yet, sometimes we need to just 'embrace the pink' and rather than apologize for it, view it as part of our uniqueness.

Clay Aiken was the runner-up in the second season of American Idol. In his book, Learning to Sing, he shares that he "did not look like the other kids" who were auditioning. Yet, his uniqueness was what made

Clay Aiken memorable. As he explains:

> "If I had looked the part, maybe I wouldn't have stuck in their minds. If I had been the same as every other boy who tried out, I would have been easier to forget. But a skinny bespectacled boy with lung power— that they remembered. It was my oddness that made me special."[2]

Clay went on to be selected as a finalist in American Idol and he won millions of viewers' votes. Simon Cowell, the uncompromising American Idol judge, said to Clay, "You know what, you may not look like a pop star, but I think that's what makes you so special."[3]

One of the things that I have discovered makes me unique is the way I speak. Not that it is particularly special. In fact, I speak much the same as the other twenty million Australians around the world. It seems that wherever I am in America someone asks me where I am from. Thankfully, I enjoy meeting people and have had many engaging conversations with people.

But, there can be a downside. Sometimes, when I go through the drive-thru, the cars behind get frustrated with me because I am having trouble making myself understood. Last week, I received two tostadas instead of two soft tacos.

Once when I was having lunch with my friend, Louise, the waitress who took my order said, "I could listen to you talk all day." It was a startling comment and I'm sure she was just a little too enthusiastic. But she did get me thinking.

Maybe this is part of the unique calling that God has on me: to communicate with people. If people are willing to listen, then I need to have something to say that is worth hearing.

As more opportunities to speak with people are opened to me, I find myself encouraged by this verse:

> "But how can people call for help if they
> don't know who to trust? And how can they
> know who to trust if they haven't heard of
> the One who can be trusted? And how can
> they hear if nobody tells them?"
> (Romans 10:14 The Message)

This is what I believe that God has created me to do: to tell people of "the One who can be trusted." And as I step out in fulfilling this calling, I am experiencing His joy.

While I was busy looking at another person's gifts and capabilities, I was at risk of completely missing God's purposes for me. God does not have a 'one size fits all' purpose; He has a unique purpose for each of us. God does not call us to be accountable for anything other than what He has called us to be.

I was nineteen when I attended an event where a young girl shared a wonderful and moving song with an audience. As she introduced the song, she talked about God's provision in her life and how this particular song was a testimony of God's goodness. I was impacted by her song and her testimony and felt compelled that this was what I was called to do with my life.

After I married Wes, I was certain our passion for music and each other was perfect. I had visions of us sharing the message of Jesus through music. It was not to be. I was intimidated by Wes' musical abilities and found myself shrinking back. When he finally encouraged me to sing with him, I was terrified.

My fear of failing and lack of confidence frustrated both of us. If it had been something I was called to do, suggested Wes, then surely it would be accompanied by more joy. I think I may have slammed a door after that comment!

But, he was right! While I enjoyed singing as part of a group or a choir, I did not enjoy being a soloist. I was not even that accomplished. I realized that I might have misunderstood the sense of compulsion I had felt when I heard that girl sing many years ago.

In recent years, I have realized that what I sensed was, in fact, something God had placed on my life. But it had less to do with singing and more to do with communicating a message. When I heard that young girl communicating through singing, I had never before heard women speakers sharing God's love in a compelling manner. Since then, speakers such as Holly Wagner, Patsy Clairmont and Joyce Meyer have inspired me to be an effective communicator.

Recently, Angie recorded a CD of praise and worship songs. I was invited to sing the backing vocals. It was hard work. As we left the studio after a day of recording my vocals, I was exhausted. When we went out to get some dinner, I could barely muster the energy to join in the conversation.

Later that evening, I commented to Wes that I never feel that worn out when I speak before a group of people. In fact, such an outpouring of concentration and effort usually energizes me. Wes said something about maybe that is what I am called to do because of the joy I experience when I speak. Yes, he was right again.

There is a deep, satisfying joy that comes when we are fulfilling the purpose for which God has called us. It is not found by looking at what God is doing through someone else, but seeing what God wants to do through you. It is allowing God to use your unique gifts and abilities to reveal His calling on you. And being true to that calling is the surest way to joy.

10

Good Medicine

A sense of humor. . . is needed armor.
Joy in one's heart and some laughter on
one's lips is a sign that the person deep
down has a pretty good grasp of life.
Hugh Sidey

It is said that children laugh about two hundred
times a day. Adults laugh only fifteen times a day. It
seems the stresses of life and all of our responsibilities
which impact so much of our lives, reduce the number
of times we laugh. Sad, really.

In all of my life, I have never considered myself better
than average in any area until now. I think I am doing
better than the average for the number of times of

daily laughter. Not that I have any documented proof of this. All I know is that I do laugh a lot.

Perhaps I have never experienced the kind of tragedies so many have had to deal with. Maybe, I have less stress and therefore, more opportunities to have a sense of levity. Or maybe, I surround myself with a lot of funny people. According to Victor Borge, "Laughter is the shortest distance between two people." I know that my favorite people to spend time with are the ones with whom I share many laughs.

Angie and I are always laughing. I think in just one afternoon together we can easily surpass the average daily quota of laughs for an adult. We can always find something to laugh about even if it is just entertaining to us!

Recently, Angie and I were shopping for swimsuits. Just knowing that I need to purchase a swimsuit is enough for me to swear off chocolate for at least an hour or two! Shopping for a swimsuit and keeping your self esteem in tact requires a lot of skill. And laughter.

On this occasion, Angie and I had laughed our way through trying on many different styles and sizes of swimsuits. We each had a stack of rejected swimsuits piled high in our dressing rooms. As we were preparing to return the offending swimsuits to the racks, a lady stepped out of a nearby dressing room and said, "I want to go shopping with you two. You make it sound like so much fun."

Perhaps more challenging is to laugh in stressful situations. Some years ago, Maureen and I traveled to Australia together to attend the Hillsong conference in Sydney. We rented a car and I drove us around Sydney sharing the sights with Maureen.

One morning, we came to the toll lanes on one of the freeways and we entered the lane that required you to give the exact amount of change for the toll.

Maureen, still unfamiliar with Australian currency which uses coins for any amount less than five dollars, had to sort through our collection of American and Australian coins, adding one coin at a time in hopes of making the required amount. The more cars that joined the ever-increasing line of cars behind us, the more we laughed at the situation. Finally, a supervisor from a nearby tollbooth paid the outstanding thirty cents and sent us on our way.

My sons, David and Zachary, make me laugh. When they were little, they made me laugh with their antics. A funny face, an attempt to dance or hide, or a mispronounced word would frequently cause me to laugh out loud. Now, that they are older, David and Zachary have worked out how to make me laugh with a well-timed comment.

Recently, Wes and I took Zachary to a department store to buy some new clothes. He was accompanying Wes on a business trip and all the clothes that Zack owned were suitable for the home, not for a business event.

Wes selected some navy blue dress pants, a collared shirt and, much to Zack's horror, a tie. I waited outside the dressing room as Wes helped Zack into the world of business attire.

Finally, Zachary stepped out of the dressing room and he looked adorable. Zack sensed that he was about to be the recipient of some embarrassing motherly affection. He looked at me with a deadpan expression and said, "Does this make me look fat?"

Humans are the only species to laugh. A dog may wag his tail to express happiness, but a person has the ability to produce a laugh that may range from a giggle, to a chuckle, a chortle, or even a guffaw (yes, it's a real word). Laughter and humor are products of being made in God's image. He created us to laugh.

In fact, laughing is good for us. Paul Antokolsky, a certified laugh leader (who knew there was such a thing), explains that when you laugh,

> "You're getting oxygen into all the cells in
> your body, which is something we need for
> energy and vitality. And as a result, you're
> lowering your blood pressure, you're reducing
> your pain levels, you're even helping your
> cholesterol."[1]

The value of laughing is so well researched, there are even websites dedicated to the health benefits of laughter. As it says in Proverbs 17:22, "A cheerful heart is good medicine."

Laughter yoga clubs are being formed around the world. At these classes, people gather to intentionally laugh and so gain the desired health benefits. It seems that the stresses of modern life hinders people's ability to laugh spontaneously and so these laughter yoga clubs provide a place for people to practice laughing.

Laughter is vocalized joy. It is evidence of feeling light-hearted. It expresses joy and has a contagious quality. It tells people around you that life is giving you cause to be joyful.

There may be times when life does not give you reason to laugh. Your experience of trials and sorrow may be such that you feel you will never laugh again. In a season of sorrow, it is likely that you may not feel like laughing, but do not allow sadness and despair to take up permanent residence in your life. Allow yourself room to feel joy and to laugh again, and to regain the strength that comes from God.

A Reason to Laugh

When I was teaching, there was a game the children in my grade two class loved to play. It was a silly game that was fun during transitions from one activity to another. A few children, whose goal was to be the last to laugh, would line up along the front of the class and then other children were selected to do their best to make them laugh. There was no tickling allowed, but funny faces were definitely permissible.

It was not long before the stern expressions of the children were replaced with peals of laughter. There is nothing like the sound of a classroom of happy, laughing children.

As we get older, we are not as a quick to laugh out loud. If life has drained us of joy, laughing seems near impossible. Even a toothless, seven year old making a funny face can not make us laugh. Although that may be just what is needed.

Wes and I have been through seasons when there has been little reason to laugh. A few summers ago, there seemed to be no end to the challenges. One thing on top of another was weighing our hearts down.

In the midst of the burdensome challenges, Wes was out running one afternoon and he was attacked and bitten by a Rottweiler dog. Less than a month later, the vehicle Wes was driving was sandwiched in a four car pile-up on one of LA's busiest freeways. He injured his ribs and was uncomfortable for many weeks.

Despite our efforts, we struggled to emerge from this black cloud that seemed to hover overhead. One afternoon, Wes suggested we take a ride on his Harley. Even though his ribs were still tender, we surmised that doing something fun together would do us both good. Feeling revived by the trip, we returned home.

Because of the injury to his ribs, Wes was slower than usual to get the motorcycle into position before I proceeded to climb off. His injured ribs prevented him from being able to steady the bike. Down it came.

My leg was pinned between the fallen motorcycle and the concrete driveway. I was in pain, but worse was a sense that, yet again, things were not going well. In exasperation at our situation, Wes simply said, "Look at us. We're pathetic."

We both found that funny. It seemed the harder we were trying, the more of a mess we were creating. After spending months frustrated by our situation, we decided to just laugh at ourselves.

We both hobbled through the remainder of that summer, and while the challenges were still present, we chose to laugh in the midst of the mess. I certainly found myself agreeing with comedian, Bill Cosby, who once said, "If you can find humor in anything, you can survive it."

Shout for Joy

Sometimes, we need to act joyful even when we feel devoid of joy. Expressing joy can be a physical act. In the Bible, we are reminded to "shout to God with cries of joy" (Psalm 47:1), "go out in joy" (Isaiah 55:12), and to "ever sing for joy" (Psalm 5:11). As we express joy, somehow our feelings catch up.

The cartoon character, Charlie Brown, who is known for his 'the glass is half-empty' view of life, knew the connection between our physical actions and the way we feel. In one cartoon, Charlie Brown suggested:

"When you are depressed, it makes a lot of

difference how you stand. The worst thing
you can do is straighten up and hold your
head up high because then you'll start to feel
better."

That being said, the best way to experience joy is to
hold your head up, look up and remember to celebrate
God's love and goodness.

A good reminder to act joyful even when we feel joyless is found in Isaiah 54. Here, a barren woman, the
subject of much scorn and isolation in those times, is
commanded to: "Sing, O barren woman. . . burst into
song, shout for joy" (Isaiah 54:1).

She probably would have preferred to retreat into
her feelings of self-pity and despair but she is commanded to rejoice. Why? Because, as the prophet
announced: "Make your tents large. Spread out! Think
big! . . . You're going to need lots of elbow room for
your growing family" (Isaiah 54:4 The Message).

The fulfillment of that prophecy required her to
rejoice first. She needed to celebrate first, in spite of
her circumstances. Then God would fulfill His
promise.

Sometimes, we need to express our joy, not because
our current circumstances are conducive to celebration
but because God is faithful and we know He will keep

JOY!

His promises. Sing for joy, shout for joy, even laugh
out loud and remind yourself that with God, tomorrow
can be better than today. Remember that because of
God's faithfulness, we can "laugh at the days to come"
(Proverbs 31:25).

11

Wide Open Spaces

Joy is not in things; it is in us.
Richard Wagner
(1813-1883)

The road to my parents' home follows the coastline as it winds south. It is a picturesque drive. It has some of Australia's most rugged coastline with green hills atop treacherous hillsides which lead down to the ocean. On these hills, there are cows chewing their cud oblivious to the prime real estate they are occupying.

I love that journey. The beauty and the openness often causes me to sigh in wistful wonder. Life it seems can crowd in on us and stifle us. We have a limited view and often feel confined and restricted. Seeing those green hills and the vast expanse of ocean, I long for a life of wide, open spaces: a life that I believe God wants each of us to experience.

In Job 36:16, it is said of God that, "He is wooing you from the jaws of distress to a spacious place free of restriction." That is a wonderful picture of God calling us out from restriction and distress to a spacious place. How can we experience such a place?

Generosity Enlarges

One of the keys to being rescued from our small lives into the largeness of a life God intends for us, is to be generous. In Proverbs, it says, "The world of the generous gets larger and larger, the world of the stingy gets smaller and smaller" (Proverbs 11:24 The Message).

As we give generously, we reach beyond our own life and our own world. It causes us to consider the needs of another. It causes us to take an interest in the events outside of our own small existence. As Randy Alcorn says in *The Treasure Principle*, "Giving infuses life with joy. It interjects eternal dimension into even the most ordinary day."[1]

Recently, I heard Gracia Burnham, whom I wrote about in chapter 5, being interviewed on *The 700 Club*. While Gracia and Martin were held hostage in the Philippines, there had been many people who wanted to help them but didn't know how.

When Gracia returned to the United States and was reunited with her three children, these people began to send money to her. Using this money, Gracia set up a foundation called *The Martin and Gracia Burnham Foundation* to support missionary aviation, tribal missionary work and Christian ministries to Muslims. In the interview, Gracia described how she distributed these funds saying, "It has been so much fun to give and give."[2]

What an expansive way to live! Gracia Burnham has experienced dreadful hardships and tragedy, yet when she spoke of giving, her face lit up. Rather than dwelling on all she had lost, Gracia was celebrating all she could give. She is a testimony to these words of Jesus: "It is more blessed to give than to receive" (Acts 20:35).

As a family, we give first to our church and then to other charities and organizations such as Compassion, Samaritan's Purse and Voice of the Martyrs. What I notice is that I become very interested in what is being done by those organizations that we support. As we give, we participate in their work around the world.

With so many great causes to give to, sometimes it is hard to know how to give more. Sometimes, we need to be creative. This is something I do for an organization called The Gleanings for the Hungry. Based in Northern California, this organization dries fruits and vegetables to send overseas to feed those living in poverty.

The name, Gleanings, is taken from the Old Testament. According to the law at that time, the harvesters would leave a little of their crop in the fields to be picked up by the poor. In this way, the poor could glean the fields and gather some food for their families.

So, at the end of the week, I gather the loose change from my purse and place it in a large glass jar. Each Christmas, I empty that jar and send the money to Gleanings. Often, it is only forty dollars but I get such joy when I read their newsletters and see photos of children enjoying some dried fruit or soup made with dried vegetables.

As we give, we are investing beyond ourselves. It helps us to realize our abundance. It allows us to reach beyond our world to make a difference in someone else's world.

Zachary, demonstrated this big thinking recently. Wes and I do not give our sons gifts of money. If they want money, they know to ask for a job so that they can earn money. Even birthdays do not bring gifts of money. On Zack's birthday, a friend gave him a bag of candy with a five dollar bill. He treasured that unexpected blessing and tucked it into his wallet. He began to plan how to use that money.

Less than two weeks later, the tragedy of the tsunami impacted nations around the world. Now, Zack knew exactly what he wanted to do with his money. Without any prompting from his parents, Zack gave his five dollars to Samaritan's Purse to help in their relief efforts.

Too often, we believe that giving means less for us. But that is not the case. The more we give, the more we receive because we demonstrate to God our willingness to be used to bless others. We become a channel through which God's blessings can flow to others.

I like the advice of this verse: "Giving not getting is the way. Generosity begets generosity. Stinginess impoverishes" (Mark 4:25 The Message). As we give generously, we experience the joy of feeling connected to something bigger than our own world. We experience a life lived in a spacious place.

Gratitude Expands

One of the first words we teach our babies in Australia is the word "Ta" meaning thank you. It is easier to say than thank you so by the time your child has mastered his or her first words, it is likely that he or she can say, "Ta." If you are a parent, it is likely that you have spent a lot of time teaching your child to say thank you. It is evident that gratitude is an important value.

In seeking an expansive life, we need to consider the place of gratitude. Without gratitude, we fail to recognize all that we have been given. Without an attitude of gratitude, we are likely to overlook the blessings and provision of God in our life. As someone once said, "Hem your blessings with gratitude so they don't unravel."

When we fail to be thankful for what we have, we can too easily be fixated on what we don't possess. Our vision becomes limited to what we lack. Gratitude expands our life because it reminds us to be thankful for all that we have been given. As the hymn says: "Count your blessings name them one by one and it will surprise you what the Lord has done."

In Philippians 4, Paul, when reminding people to pray, wrote:

> "Do not be anxious about anything, but in everything, by prayer and petition *with thanksgiving*, present your requests to God."
> (Philippians 4:6, italics added)

It is important to remember to maintain a spirit of gratitude lest, when we pray, we sound like a demanding child in a store.

My son, David, has a grateful heart. Now that he is in Junior High, his social life is requiring me to drive him around town. Every time I pick him up from a basketball game or an outing, he always thanks me. He knows that he needs me to play a role in making his social life happen. He is looking beyond himself and remembering to thank me, the taxi driver!

So too, when we pray with a heart of thanksgiving, we're acknowledging the role that God has in our life. We're expanding our vision of our life to see the presence and provision of our Heavenly Father. That will definitely lead us to a spacious place where we can experience joy. I like Chuck Swindoll's perspective on this. He says, "Joy becomes a transaction between you and God that other's can't help but notice. It's God's life spilling over the brim of your life and into other's lives." [3]

By bringing to mind things we are thankful for, it helps us to remember what God has done. It seems we readily remember the bad things of life but we let the good things, the things we should be grateful for, slip from our minds. I remember talking with David one night about prayer and he asked me if God had ever answered any of my prayers. My answer: "Of course."

"When?" asked David. Don't you love those late night challenges from your teenager!

Trying to bring examples to mind, I noticed that I was faltering. If David had asked me about prayers that I'm still waiting to be answered, I could have run through that list effortlessly. After a few moments, my memory brought to light examples of answered prayers. The conversation ended well. David's curiosity had been satisfied, but I came away with the realization that I wanted to "forget not all his benefits" (Psalm 103:2).

It seems Moses, too, was concerned about people's propensity to forget all that God had done. And God had done so much for the Israelites. He had rescued them from slavery in Egypt, led them for forty years in the desert, provided manna and water, and, according to the Bible, prevented their shoes and clothes from wearing out (What! No shopping!). Moses' warning to the people of Israel is worth heeding today:

> "Only be careful and watch yourselves closely
> so that you do not forget the things you have
> seen or let them slip from your heart as long
> as you live. Teach them to your children and
> to their children after them." (Deuteronomy
> 4:9)

Remembering God's goodness, His faithfulness, His love, mercy and grace will keep us from living a limited, shallow life. Instead, with gratitude, we can expand our vision and see God at work. We can dive into the depths of experiencing His joy.

12

Deflating Joy

God created us in joy and for joy, and in the long
run not all the darkness there is in the world and
in ourselves can separate us finally from that joy,
because whatever else it means to say God created
us in his image. . . his mark is deep within us.
We have God's joy in our blood.
Frederick Buechner

Nothing will deflate our joy more quickly than fear
and worry. Fear and worry are not given to us from
God. As we read in James, "every good and perfect gift
comes from God" (James 1:17). So where does fear and
worry come from? They are the tactics of the thief who
wants to steal your joy.

Unfortunately, I can easily surrender my joy to fear and worry. When I allow myself to entertain fearful and anxious thoughts, I quickly forget that neither comes from God. In those times, my joy can be deflated and my strength drains rapidly away.

Fear Saps Joy

A friend once told me that there are 365 commands in the Bible to 'fear not' or to be courageous. That's one command for every day of the year. And it sometimes seems like I need every one.

Fear can loom large in our lives. Patsy Clairmont says, in her book, *I Grew Up Little*, "a fear is nothing more than a tangle of feelings. But when those feelings determine the choices we make, they can become full-blown phobias."[1] What a good reminder that fear should not have such a hold in our lives; this tangle of feelings should not warrant our attention or determine our actions.

Fear can gain power in our life. I remember when Zachary was young he hated to be upstairs alone in our house. For whatever reason, he would not go upstairs without first asking if anyone else was up there. Some days, Zachary would stand at the bottom of the stairs and plead with me to go with him.

One day, I was out and Zachary was at home with Wes and David. Wes was busy working in the office and Zack needed to get some socks which were in his bedroom upstairs. No amount of talking or coaxing would convince Zack to go up the stairs alone. The thing about fear is that it can too easily intimidate us, demotivate us and immobilize us.

In the middle of Wes' best motivational message for a four year old, I phoned the house to check in. Wes told me of Zack's dilemma and asked me to speak with him. I told Zack if he continued to speak with me on the phone while he went upstairs, it would be like I am there with him.

Clutching the cordless phone to his ear, Zack made the long trek up the stairs to his bedroom, opened the drawer and picked out a pair of socks. With my voice assuring him that there was nothing to fear, Zack was able to move forward. (Now, that would make a good commercial for a phone company!)

When we are immobilized by fear, we fail to move forward. We can miss out on living an expansive life because we allow ourselves to be restricted by fear. We limit God's work in our lives. That's a high price for harboring a few fears.

We need to listen for God's voice. As the Bible reminds us, "God is our refuge and strength, an ever present help in trouble. Therefore we will not fear. . ." (Psalm 46:1-2)

If there is one fear I have to work hard to overcome, it is the dreaded fear of what people may think or say about me. Some never struggle with this fear; for others, like me, this fear can suck the joy right out of life. I recall a time when I almost let that fear prevent me from experiencing God's best for my life.

When I was nineteen, after just six months of dating, Wes proposed marriage. Four times. Now the way Wes tells it, it sounds like I was playing hard to get. Let me set the record straight.

The night Wes proposed, he caught me completely off guard. In fact, when he 'popped the question', I laughed. Not exactly a moment Wes would refer to as one of the high points in our unfolding love story.

What Wes often neglects to share is that when he proposed marriage, I was still living at home with my parents and in my second year of college. That evening, I had just shared with him my career plans, including the contingency plan to be a nanny in England if the shortage of teaching positions in Australia continued. Wes' proposal was very surprising.

Certainly, not a laughing matter. But my nervous surprise manifested itself as a laugh.

Undeterred by my laugh, Wes proposed a second time. My response: "Let me think about it." Hardly the most romantic response but I really did want to think about it. This was a big step. Marrying Wes meant moving to a city two hours away from my family, becoming a pastor's wife, transferring colleges and maybe, even moving to the United States in the future. I had a lot to think about.

I also had started to wonder what people would think of me marrying so young. Wes and I had only been together for six months, and he was overseas for two of those months. I would be the first of my siblings to marry and the first in my circle of friends to marry. What would they say?

One of my favorite Proverbs states: "The fear of the human opinion disables" (Proverbs 29:25 The Message). How true. Our fear of what they (whoever they are) may think or say can stop us in our tracks. Whether it is to pursue a dream, do something new, or even to break out of a fashion rut, we can fear people's opinions and end up doing nothing.

A week after proposals number one and two, Wes asked me again to marry him. This time I said, yes but

with a conditional clause that we not tell anyone.
Who does that? Someone who is letting fear hold
them back.

Another week passed. I think Wes wasn't particularly
pleased with how this scenario was unfolding. So this
time, he issued an ultimatum: either we get married or
he was moving on. He gave me a week to think it
through.

My initial response was anger. How dare he! But
then again, none of this had gone as he had planned. I
knew I loved Wes and wanted to spend the rest of my
life with him. It was just a very big and scary step.

The rest of Proverbs 29:25 says; "The fear of the
human opinion disables, trusting in God protects you
from that." I needed to seek God's wisdom. This
decision was going to require me to be less concerned
with people's thoughts and more concerned with
God's mind on the matter.

As I trusted in God, I sensed confidence in the
thought of marrying Wes. Because of Wes' adventurous
spirit, it would mean signing up for a less predictable
and safe life. Yet, because of his passion for the Lord,
I knew I would have a life partner whose priorities
would be the same as mine. I knew there was no one
I'd rather be with and so, finally, I said yes. That was

twenty wonderful years ago (except for that one night in a trailer in Mexico).

Whatever your fears, do not allow them to hold you back from God's best for you. I almost allowed my fear to lead me away from the joy of a life that God had in store for me.

Counter fear with faith. As someone once said, "Feed your faith and your fears will starve to death." I like the words of Proverbs 19:23: "The fear of the Lord leads to life: Then one rests content, untouched by trouble." Move away from fear toward life. Keep trusting in God because He wants to fill your life with His joy.

Worry Drains Joy

At different times, David and Zachary have kept pet hamsters. We have owned a few of these cute, furry creatures. There's been Lucy, Annie, Mary, and Lily. Currently, we have Peaches residing with us. As far as pets go, hamsters are relatively low maintenance.

There's one thing that each of these hamsters have had in common. In the quiet hours of the night, hamsters run for hours on the exercise wheel in their cage.

It seems this is the preferred workout for hamsters; spinning aimlessly on a wheel that is going no where. And yet, every night, they run unperturbed by their lack of progress.

Much as I like to laugh at the hamsters' antics, I have sometimes been engaged in an activity that is equally futile. Sometimes, in the quiet hours of the night, I let the wheels of my mind spin as I worry. It seems I have plenty to worry about at night: the boys' education, the boys' health, Wes' health, my health, the state of the economy, and the list goes on. All these worries accomplish nothing.

I like what author and pastor, Max Lucado, has to say on this subject. In his book, *Traveling Light*, he writes:

> "Worry divides the mind. The biblical word for worry (merimnao) is a compound of two Greek words, merizo ('to divide') and nous ('the mind'). Anxiety splits our energy between today's priorities and tomorrow's problems. Part of our mind is on the now; the rest is on the not yet. The result is half-minded living."[2]

One of the ways we can experience joy is to savor the moment. With "half-minded living," as Max Lucado calls it, we are depriving ourselves of the joy that can be experienced in that moment.

When we have little children, we can, too easily, worry away those precious years as we worry about their health, their development and their future. Yet, as they get older, we may still be anxious about those same things. By the time they are leaving for college, we may spend our time worrying about their choices. It seems our days, and especially nights, are filled with worrying about scenarios that may never happen.

From his jail cell, Paul wrote: "Do not fret or worry. Instead of worrying, pray" (Philippians 4:4 The Message). I have found that prayer is the best remedy to worry. In those futile hours of worrying, I have to climb off the spinning wheels of worry, which will accomplish nothing, and choose to pray for whatever concerns me. As Mary C. Crowley once said, "Every evening I turn my worries over to God. He's going to be up all night anyway."

Some nights, I will pray and whatever was filling me with anxiety diminishes and I fall asleep. I used to be so disappointed in myself for falling asleep mid-prayer. I know I wouldn't like to be engaged in a conversation with someone while they drift to sleep. Some years ago, I found this verse which says, "for he grants sleep to those he loves" (Psalm 127:2). God's peaceful sleep is a gift. He intends for us to rest and to not waste our energy on unproductive anxiety.

Further on in Philippians 4, Paul writes, "It's wonderful what happens when Christ displaces worry at the center of your life" (4:7 The Message). It would be such a waste of all that we have been given if we allow worry to be the center and so displace the joy that comes from Jesus.

Do not allow worry such a prominent position in your life. It is hardly deserving of such a role. As you worry less and pray more, you will further enjoy God's peace and presence. As Chuck Swindoll says, "When you trust Christ with the details of your life, you experience His life in wonderful excess, and it can't help but give you reason to smile."[3]

13

Fading Joy

Joy is a sustained sense of well-being and
internal peace— a connection to what matters.[1]
Oprah Winfrey

One sure way to cause joy to lose its luster, is to fail
to take the time to replenish and refresh our joy.
Without periods of rest and recreation, our harried
lives can hinder our joy. We can, too easily, find ourselves burdened and exhausted with hardly the energy
to muster a joyful heart.

Busyness is one of the symptoms of our culture. We
are all rushing somewhere. There never seems to be
enough hours in the day to do all that needs to be

done. We write 'to do' lists and at the end of the day, there are numerous tasks that are yet undone and need to be transferred onto the list for the next day.

Sometime ago, Maureen and I had taken our kids to the home of another friend. Because we homeschooled our children, we had decided to meet so that they could work on a craft activity, and spend some time playing together.

Another mutual friend dropped by to pick up something and saw Maureen and me sitting, drinking coffee and supervising the craft activity. We invited her to join us but she instead listed all that she yet needed to do, including picking up her kids from school. Then she finished by saying, "You see, I'm busy."

The way that she announced "I'm busy" was a declaration. It was inferring to us that she was doing something valuable and we were not. It was as if she was pointing to her busyness as a badge of honor. Her busyness gave her a sense of value. She was needed. She was busy.

Too often, I do the exact same thing. I feel a need to justify all that I do with an announcement of my busyness. It is almost as if I'm afraid that I'll be accused of laziness. I would prefer to burn out with exhaustion than to be accused of being lazy.

Fading Joy

Busyness often arises simply because we are products of a society that offers so much opportunity to be engaged in life. There are experiences and opportunities around every corner. And there is a lot of temptation and cultural pressure to do it all and have it all.

When I was nine, I asked my parents if I could play competition netball (the ball game of choice for young girls in Australia). My parents could not afford to own a car, and so they did not have a car. To lease a car was not an option available to them.

Since they had no means to transport me to and from practices and games, their decision was simple: I could not play netball. Today, everyone owns at least one car and there are weekend games of baseball, soccer and basketball offered for every age. How can we refuse the offers?

There is so much pressure on parents to provide their children with the best opportunities to excel in anything. We are certain that if we don't sign our children up to play baseball when they are four, there will be no chance they will reach the professional league.

David has loved playing basketball ever since he received his first basketball hoop when he was two years old. He loves to play the game, watch the game and discuss the game. Wes and I decided that he would have to wait until he was twelve years old to join a basketball team.

Our evaluations had led us to the conclusion that children who play organized sports when they are very young, often burn out by the time they are teenagers. We wanted David to wait, lest the enjoyment of playing on a team subside at a time when it would be most helpful for a teenage boy to enjoy partcipation in team activities. So, for years, David would shoot hoops everyday and practice lay-ups and free throws alone in the backyard.

Finally, David joined a basketball team. He spent the first few games trying to work out his position and find his place as a team player. By the end of the season, David was put in as one of the starting five players. Because he works hard at every practice, the coach commends his enthusiasm and dedication. While the schedule of practices and games keeps me driving back and forth across town, it is worth it because I know David's love and enjoyment for playing with a team is not waning.

Perhaps, what creates so much activity in our lives is our inability to say 'no'. Our children want to play sports, join dance classes, attend tutoring, take music lessons, visit friends, and go places. We don't want to deprive them of anything so we say 'yes'. Then we are asked to volunteer to help so we say 'yes'. Before long, we are rushing to the store to pick up snacks, dropping off kids and attending games on opposite sides of town. It is a frantic flurry of activity.

In those times when I am afforded opportunities to get involved and add one more thing to my schedule, I keep in mind the words of author and leadership instructor, John C. Maxwell, who advised: "Learn to say 'no' to the good so you can say 'yes' to the best."

Whereas at one time in my life I may have been confronted by a choice between something good and something bad, I find more and more my choices are between something good and another good thing. These are tough choices and it may require us to say 'no' to some good things.

But I like the idea of saying 'yes' to the best. What is best may be something that will benefit the whole family and not just one family member. What is best may be to stop doing something that is bringing too much pressure to an already busy schedule. What is best may be to simply wait and not rush into committing to do something more. What is best may be choosing to live with less.

Against the Flow

One Friday evening Wes, David, Zachary and I were heading down the mountain after a few nights away. Homeschooling the boys gives our schedule a degree of flexibility so that we can getaway mid-week. We take our school work with us and spend a few nights at our mountain cabin.

As we were traveling down the mountain, we noticed an endless stream of car headlights traveling up the mountain for the weekend. Sometimes I feel like my life is like that; it is moving against the flow.

Going against the flow means I have chosen not to get a position in the education field but to homeschool David and Zachary. By not putting David in a public high school, his opportunities to attract a basketball scholarship may be reduced. In a culture that says we can afford to upgrade our house and cars by increasing our debt, we have chosen to be content with all we have and not incur additional debt. Our desire to say yes to the best has meant we have often gone against the flow.

In Romans 12:2, it says: "Do not conform any longer to the pattern of this world but be transformed by the renewing of your mind." The pattern of this world says I must prove my worth by being busy and productive. It says if my kids do not excel in sports and academics, then they will have a less promising future. The pattern of this world says that I can have it all and do it all now.

In renewing our minds, we strive to bring our thinking more closely into line with God's thoughts. His thoughts are that we don't have to prove our value but that "there is no condemnation for those who are in Christ Jesus" (Romans 8:1).

Academic excellence and sporting prowess may have some value in this world, but raising kids with a heart for Jesus and a desire to serve Him is more valuable than anything. God's plan for each child is "to prosper you and not to harm you, plans to give you a hope and a future" (Jeremiah 29:11). God's view of our life is that "my grace is sufficient for you, for my power is made perfect in weakness" (2 Corinthians 12:9).

Someone once said, that if Satan can't make us bad, he can make us busy. I suspect we are more than capable of making ourselves busy with very little help from anyone. If we allow ourselves to be caught in the flow of this world's direction, we may discover our schedule is crammed full and our 'to do' list is overwhelming.

Lives full of activity can become lives that crowd out joy. As we become caught up in what we need to do, we can easily neglect our relationship with the One who did it all for us. As we hurriedly rush from activity to activity because it all depends on us, we can ignore the voice of the One upon whom we can depend.

Psalm 46:10 says, "Be still and know that I am God." Sometimes we allow ourselves to become so busy that we don't even have time to be still. Yet, it is in the times of being still we are reminded of the presence of the One who fills us with joy.

Restored Joy

Busy lives can lead to joyless lives. Frantic rushing to meet deadlines, to make appointments on time, and to fulfill all of our commitments can cause us to feel overwhelmed and harried. We leave little space in our schedules to re-connect with God. Yet it is often in the quiet that we find God's presence. That was the experience of Elijah, the Old Testament prophet.

Elijah met on Mount Carmel for a showdown with King Ahab and the prophets of the pagan god, Baal. For hours, the 450 prophets cried, shouted and danced around an altar imploring Baal to consume their offering with fire. Their sacrifice was not touched.

Elijah drenched the altar with water. He then stood before the sacrifice and prayed to God. The sacrifice was consumed by fire from heaven. It was a spectacular event.

Ahab's wife wanted Elijah punished because he had disgraced and killed the prophets of Baal. Fearing for his life, Elijah fled to the desert where he hid in a cave. It was there that he had an encounter with God.

God told Elijah that His presence would pass by him. First, there was a powerful wind, an earthquake and then a fire, but God's presence was not there. Then came a gentle whisper. It was here that Elijah met God.

Despite the spectacular event at Mount Carmel, and the wind, the earthquake and fire at the cave, God came to Elijah as a gentle whisper. Sometimes we need to step back from the busyness of our lives and remove ourselves from the din long enough to re-connect with God and experience His presence.

In Psalm 23, David provides an analogy of God as our shepherd who "makes me lie down in green pastures, he leads me beside quiet waters" (Psalm 23:2-3).

JOY!

It is a peaceful scene that brings a sense of refreshment and renewal. We need moments like that in our lives; moments of resting by quiet waters. It is in those moments, we can best hear the gentle whisper of God.

It is so easy to be led by the hurrying pace of our culture. But sometimes, I need to remind myself to go against the flow, say yes to God's best and let the Good Shepherd lead me to a place where He can "restore my soul" (Psalm 23:3). As I take moments to be still, I allow God to remove the tarnish that conceals my joy. He will, in those pauses in life, restore my joy and reveal its brilliance.

14

Overflowing Joy

I have told you these things so
that you will be filled with my joy.
Yes, your joy will overflow.
(John 15:11 NLT)

After Angie and I had been friends for only two years, her husband's work required the family to re-locate to the San Fernando valley. Because she lived across the other side of LA, or as my kids used to say, 'five freeways away', Angie and I would attempt to meet up every three to four months at some place equal distance from each of us. Most times, it was a place that was suitable for the kids like a park. On this occasion, we planned a night out for just the two of us.

Amy Grant was going to be performing a Christmas concert in Anaheim. We decided this would be a great place to catch up on each other's lives and to enjoy some good music. During the concert, we were enjoying each other's company, talking and laughing while listening to the music (a typical case of females multitasking). All the while, we were unaware that our enjoyment was bothering someone.

Midway through the song, *Sleigh Ride*, a lady seated in the row in front of us, turned around and said sternly, "Look, I did not pay good money to listen to you two talk and laugh all night." Feeling a little embarrassed by our scolding, Angie and I tried to be more sensitive to those around us so we limited our talking and refrained from outbursts of laughter.

Sometimes joy is like that. An abundance of joy can overflow. Unable to be contained, joy spills out and your joy may spill onto others nearby. Of course, it is best if it is going to be well received: people savoring the sweet melodies of a Christmas concert may not be in need of my overflowing joy. But there are other situations were a splash of joy would be refreshing and appreciated.

overflowing Joy

Contagious Joy

After living in the United States for two years, Wes started the process of changing our immigration status so that we could qualify for green cards. It was a complicated and time consuming process, especially because Wes wanted to save the expense of hiring an immigration attorney. After numerous phone calls to the Immigration and Naturalization Services in LA, and completing reams of paper work, Wes had an interview at the INS office.

The interview was successful. Wes, without the help of an attorney, was awarded a green card and his passport was stamped verifying his new status. There was just one more detail he needed to work out. Wes asked the immigration officer, "What about my wife and two sons?"

In his phone conversations with the INS staff, Wes had been advised to not start the process of upgrading his family's status until he had been assured of his green card. No one had informed Wes that the visa that allowed his family to remain in the country up to this time would be considered obsolete once he was given a green card. In stamping Wes' passport with his new status, the boys and I were suddenly made illegal aliens.

When Wes came home, it was evident that something had gone wrong. He was despairing the error and the fact that I was now an illegal alien. He felt bad that a simple piece of information meant that if his family was to leave the country for any reason, we could not return. Poor Wes couldn't even celebrate his green card. He was devastated.

I thought it was funny. A friend who was visiting at the time started to joke with me that I was an illegal alien. The more we talked about the situation, the funnier it became. We entertained ourselves with ridiculous scenarios to try to resolve the problem.

Rather than burdening an already despairing Wes with my anxiety and uncertainty, I chose to laugh. By allowing my joy to overflow, it provided some much needed refreshment to Wes.

The next day, Wes and I drove to Malibu and met with immigration attorneys who were able to start the process of securing green cards for David, Zachary and me.

Three months, a few immunizations and ten thousand dollars later, our immigration status was upgraded. We are now classified as resident aliens. Go ahead, you can laugh.

overflowing Joy

Joy can be infectious. There is a song which says, "I've got joy like a fountain." Just like a fountain in a desert, a spring of joy can bring refreshment in dry and desolate times.

There is a beautiful, outdoor shopping mall in Scottsdale, Arizona where a hot summer's day can reach 115 degrees. In one section of this mall, there is a paved area where intermittent spurts of water shoot up from the ground. Giggling children run back and forth over the area hoping to be the recipient of a refreshing burst of water.

A spring of joy can be something that catches people's attention. As it says in John 15:11: "your joy will over-flow." It can be evidence of a life grounded in God. People notice that kind of joy.

Psalm 126 is a joyful psalm. It describes the return of God's people to Israel after being held as captives in a foreign land. As they returned, the people sang in celebration:

> "Our mouths were filled with laughter, our tongues with songs of joy. Then it was said among the nations, 'The Lord has done great things for them.' The Lord has done great things for us and we were filled with joy."
> (Psalm 126:2-3)

Their joy was so evident that the surrounding
nations were talking about what God had done for the
people of Israel. Their joy was so obvious that they
made an impression on others.

According to William Barclay, "A gloomy Christian
is a contradiction in terms, and nothing in all religious
history has done Christianity more harm than its
connection with black clothes and gloomy faces."

Let our joy overflow. There are people in our com-
munities who are living dry and desolate lives. They
need to experience the joy that comes from God. Let it
overflow from you to them. Live in such a way that
your joy will be noticed and appreciated.

Refilling Your Joy

It will probably come as no surprise that I love God's
Word, the Bible. I am convinced that it is the best
source for answers to every question or dilemma that
this life may bring. I read it for encouragement, for
guidance and for insight into understanding my life
and purpose. When life begins to drain my joy, God's
Word can refuel it.

Because I was raised in a pastor's home, I have

always been familiar with the Bible. I have enough Bible knowledge to answer most Bible trivia questions. I have read and re-read verses of the Bible so often that I can find them again with little effort.

I have memorized verses for as long as I remember. Mind you, my motivation for memorization was probably so that I could be rewarded with a sticker or a piece of candy. But this has nothing to do with loving God's Word.

God's Word keeps me connected with its Author. The more I read, the more I direct my thoughts towards God. His Word has been "a lamp to my feet and a light for my path" (Psalm 119:105). It is "more precious than gold. . . sweeter than honey" (Psalm 19:10). As I read, I re-discover that the Bible is "my delight" (Psalm 119:174).

There are many devotional books based on the Bible. There are many books that teach about the Bible. But the Bible itself is like no other book. I have discovered the best way to enjoy God's Word is to just read it. Read without a sense of obligation. Read for pleasure. Keep a copy by your bed, near the kitchen counter (it's good to read with a morning cup of coffee) and in the car. As you read, you will savor the words and hear God's words for you.

JOY!

In all of life's uncertainties, all of life's trials, all of life's activity, God's Word can be a constant source of joy. It can sustain and strengthen you. As David wrote in Psalm 19: "The commandments of the Lord are right, bringing joy to the heart" (Psalm 19:8 NLT). Keeping your joy is possible when you continue to refuel on the words of God as found in the Bible.

15

A Life of Joy

You love him even though you have never seen him.
Though you do not see him now, you trust him; and
you rejoice with a glorious, inexpressible joy.
(I Peter 1:8 NLT)

My mother tells me that I was a happy baby. Happy and sleepy. It was probably a good combination. It was a difficult period for my mother's family. Supposedly, I was a joyful distraction in their home. Because of my happy disposition and because my middle name is Joy, I was called Joybells.

As cute as that name may have been then, I earned that name by being a chubby, easy-going, eighteen month old baby. It did not require an intentional effort on my part. And yet, I'd like to believe I can still bring joy into a situation. I'd like to believe that I can live in such a way to radiate joy; and that my life would be one of joy.

Last summer, I was speaking with Sheila Gerald. Sheila and her husband, Kevin, are the Senior Pastors of the Champions Centre in the state of Washington. Sheila shared with me that one of her life values was energy. Basically, wherever she was, whatever situation she walked into, she wanted to bring life-giving energy. Sheila is living out that value and in one encounter with her, her energy is evident and inspiring.

I like that idea of having a life value; something that matters enough to me to warrant my intentional focus and action. If I was to define my life value, I would like it to be joy. I'd like to live in such a manner that my joy is apparent. I want my life to promote a message of joy and that the joy of the Lord would be my strength. I want to live with continuous joy.

Joy for the Journey

Consider how easily a baby smiles at a simple game of peek-a-boo, or how a toddler grins while clutching a new toy, and it seems joy is associated with youth. It seems joy is less evident as we age. Movie titles like *Grumpy Old Men* hint at this idea that the older we get, the more difficult it is to express or to experience joy.

It is easy to fall into the trap of believing the lie that as we get older, our joy will decrease. My desire is to live a life of joy until the day I leave this planet. I am intending to not let my joy fade but to let it radiate always. I share the sentiment of John Mayer's words in his song, *No Such Thing*, when he sings: "I like to think the best of me is still hiding up my sleeve."

In Isaiah 35, the prophet, Isaiah, describes what becomes of those who continue to walk along the 'Way of Holiness'. According to Isaiah, there will be abundant blessing such as streams in the desert, life changing healing, and displays of God's glory. What I love in this passage is the verse which says, "They'll sing as they make their way home to Zion, unfading halos of joy encircling their heads" (Isaiah 35:10 The Message). That's my intention— to wear an unfading halo of joy!

Pearl has an unfading halo of joy. Pearl lost her husband of fifty plus years to cancer. She was in her seventies and was suddenly without her life partner. It would have been easy for Pearl to settle into a quiet life of tending roses and little more. Instead, Pearl moved to Thailand and taught English to Thai children. She was still teaching there when she celebrated her eightieth birthday.

At a time when retirement is acceptable and even expected, Pearl continues to experience joy as she serves the needs of others. Her halo of joy has not faded.

In Psalm 92, it says of those who continue to live a life that is faithful in serving God,

> "they will flourish in the courts of our God.
> They will still bear fruit in old age, they will
> stay fresh and green. . ." (Psalm 92:13-14)

My parents, after retiring from ministry, spent six months in Botswana, Africa, teaching in a Bible college. Wes' mother recently traveled to Indonesia as part of a missions team. Like Pearl, they have continued to flourish and bear fruit. I'd like to follow their example and bear the fruit of the spirit as described in Galatians 6. I'm planning on staying 'fresh and green' with an unfading halo of joy.

Never Ending Joy

When the new millennium dawned in Australia, countries around the world watched intently. The year 2000 arrived in Sydney sixteen hours before the countdown in Times Square, in New York City. Fears of the supposed Y2K crisis dissipated as scenes of the New Year's celebrations in Sydney were televised around the world.

The Sydney Harbour Bridge was the focal point of the fireworks celebration. At the climax of the celebration, the word 'Eternity', written in a distinctive cursive style, lit up the bridge making a bold statement for all to see. It was not the first time Sydneysiders had seen that word.

It is believed that by the time Alfred Stace died in 1967, he had written the word 'Eternity' more than half a million times on the pavements of Sydney.[1] In 1930, Alfred Stace had heard a message in which a preacher declared that he wished 'eternity' could be proclaimed through the streets of Sydney.

Inspired by this message, Alfred Stace began a ritual of rising in the early hours of the morning and writing the word 'Eternity' in chalk on the sidewalks, walls and the entrances to train stations throughout Sydney. Alfred Stace became Sydney's best known graffiti artist, and his 'tag' was a reminder to the people of Sydney to consider their eternal destiny.[2]

An eternal perspective is a key to living with joy. Sometimes we need to be reminded that the promise of eternity can fill us with our greatest joy. In the midst of all that can fill our life with concerns, sorrows or tragedy, the promise of our eternal destination is the promise of never ending joy.

There can be no greater joy than to know the promise of that future home. Looking forward to eternity should fill us with comforting, abundant, and ceaseless joy. As Jesus promised his disciples, in that eternal home, "no one will take away your joy" (John 16:22).

One day, I was speaking with a lady who was living with her husband and children in one country while her parents and extended family were living in another country. She and I were talking about the challenges of being separated from family by thousands of miles of ocean. She said to me, "What I find hardest is that I always feel like my heart is divided."

I could understand her sentiment as I often feel like I have my heart in two places. Yet when I think about heaven, I know I will no longer feel like my heart is divided. There will be no more goodbyes in heaven.

Sometimes when I am with good friends or enjoying the company of family, I catch a glimpse of eternity. I imagine being in a place surrounded by loved ones. It will be a reunion like no other. It will be the biggest, loudest, most joyous celebration of all.

On the last evening of the missionary conference I attended in Europe, people were packing to return to countries all over the world. Families were discussing flight schedules and itineraries.

During the evening, we received word that the northeastern United States and Canada had been hit by a massive power blackout grounding flights to and from many airports. Suddenly flight plans were interrupted and there was much uncertainty as to how this would impact our return flights.

I was anxious to get home. I had been away from Wes, David and Zachary for over two weeks and the thought of being stranded for another day in a country so far from home did not appeal to me. Trying to be positive and speak words of faith, I said to one of the worried travelers, "Just think, we'll all be home soon."

As soon as I said those words, I felt all my anxieties fade. The truth of those words impacted me: We will be home soon. One day, we will be in that place that Jesus has been preparing for us. As he promised,

> ". . . I am on my way to get your room ready, I'll come back and get you so you can live where I live" (John 14:1-3 The Message).

What a joy it will be when we see Jesus and he takes us by the hand and says, "Welcome home!"

We will experience our greatest joy as we live in God's presence. No longer separated from our Father, we will enjoy eternity in the presence of God. As it says in the last book of the Bible:

> "Look, God's home is now among his people! He will live with them, and they will be his people. God himself will be with them. He will wipe away every tear from their eyes, and there will be no more death, or sorrow, or crying, or pain. All these things will be gone forever." (Revelation 21:3-4 NLT)

And in that place, our joy will never end!

Dear Father God,

I praise you because You are a Holy, faithful, and loving God.

Thank you for the wonderful life you have given me. Forgive me for the times I have taken for granted all of Your blessings.

Help me to live a life of joy; that my life would be a radiant testimony to others of my relationship with You. It is because of Your son, Jesus, that I can experience this complete and everlasting joy! From this moment forward, I commit to live as a better reflection of Your joy for me .

Amen.

Notes

Chapter 1: Complete Joy

1. Charles Stanley, *Walking Wisely: Real Guidance for Life's Journey* (Nashville, TN: Thomas Nelson Publishers 2002), 57.

2. Joel Osteen, *Your Best Life Now: 7 Steps to Living At Your Full Potential* (New York, NY: Warner Faith 2004), 276.

Chapter 3: Praise On!

1. Darrell Evans, "Trading My Sorrows," © copyright 1998 Integrity's Hosanna! Music/ASCAP

2. Cathy Lechner, *I'm Trying to Sit at His Feet But Who's Going to Cook Dinner* (Lake Mary, Florida: Creation House 1995) 53.

Chapter 4: Find the Fun

1. "Corporate Speakers—Gale Sayers," The Bazel Group Inc., <http://www.corporateartists.com/speaker_gayle_sayers.html>

Chapter 5: A Changed Perspective

1. Gracia Burnham with Dean Merrill, *To Fly Again: Surviving the Tailspins of Life* (Wheaton, Illinois: Tyndale House 2005), 164.

Chapter 6: Look Up!

1. Paul Thigpen, "Where's the Joy?" Discipleship Journal, Issue 93, May/June 1996.

2. Thigpen, "Where's the Joy?"

3. Oswald Chambers, as quoted by Bob and Emilie Barnes in *15 Minute Devotions for Couples* (Eugene, Oregon: Harvest House 1995), 92.

4. Brother Lawrence of the Resurrection, translated by John J. Delaney, *The Practice of the Presence of God* (New York, NY: Image Books, Doubleday 1977), 50.

Chapter 8: No Place I'd Rather Be

1. Phil Vassar and Craig Wiseman, "Just Another Day in Paradise," © copyright 2000 EMI April Music Inc.

2. Mark Reed, "Choosing Joy," Discipleship Journal, Issue 37, Jan. 1987.

3. Osteen, *Your Best Life Now*, 272.

Chapter 9: Uniquely You

1. Stacey S. Padrick "Invasion of the Joy Snatchers," Discipleship Journal, Issue 124, July/August 2001.

2. Clay Aiken, *Learning to Sing: Hearing the Music in Your Life* (New York, NY: Random House 2004), 175.

3. Aiken, *Learning to Sing*, 184.

Chapter 10: Good Medicine

1. "Research: Laughter is Good Medicine," May 10, 2004, <http://www.thebostonchannel.com/health/3288698/detail.html>

Chapter 11: Wide Open Spaces

1. Randy Alcorn, *The Treasure Principle: Discovering the Secret of Joyful Giving* (Sisters, Oregon: Multnomah Publishers 2001), 33.

2. Gracia Burnham interview with Pat Robertson on CBN's The 700 Club, April 21, 2005.

3. Chuck Swindoll, "A Reason to Smile," April 25, 2002
<http://www.oneplace.com/ministries/insight_for_living/
Article.asp?article_id=228>
Chapter 12: Deflating Joy
1. Patsy Clairmont, *I Grew Up Little: Finding Hope in a Big God*
(Nashville, TN: W. Publishing Group 2004), 97.
2. Max Lucado, *Traveling Light: Releasing the Burdens You Were Never
Intended to Bear* (Nashville TN, W. Publishing Group 2001), 48.
3. Chuck Swindoll, "A Reason to Smile," April 25, 2002
Chapter 13: Fading Joy
1. Oprah Winfrey, "What I Know For Sure," O Magazine, May 2001
Chapter 15: A Life of Joy
1. Belief in Action: Support Material for K-6 H.S.I.E. Syllabus,
"Eternity" (Sydney, NSW: Dept. of Education and Training), 10.
2. Belief in Action, "Eternity," 11.

Contact Information:

www.EllieBeavis.com

POWERBORN
631 Via Paraiso
Corona, CA USA 92882

1-877-937-2665